RACE ME
IN A
LOBSTER
SUIT

RACE ME IN A LOBSTER SUIT

ABSURD INTERNET ADS AND THE REAL CONVERSATIONS THAT FOLLOWED

Kelly Mahon

QUIRK BOOKS
PHILADELPHIA

The conversations in this book have been reproduced with the permission of the correspondents. Conversations have been lightly edited for grammar and spelling, and the names of correspondents have been changed to protect the privacy and/or dignity of the individuals.

Library of Congress Cataloging in Publication Number: 2018943039

ISBN: 978-1-68369-104-4

Printed in China
Typeset in Hand It and Plantin

Designed by Andie Reid
Illustrations by Graham Annable
Production management by John J. McGurk

Quirk Books
215 Church Street
Philadelphia, PA 19106
quirkbooks.com

10 9 8 7 6 5 4 3 2 1

FOR MY PARENTS

IF YOU THINK ABOUT IT,
THIS IS SORT OF LIKE A GRANDCHILD . . .

BOOK > CONTENTS

Talking to Strangers

You see that girl standing at the counter in the AT&T store, sweating as she tries to explain to the guy activating her SIM card why she's buying a burner phone? Yup . . . that's me. You're probably wondering how I got there, and I'm gonna tell you, of course. But first I should probably explain how this whole thing started.

Several years and a few jobs ago, I was feeling creatively unfulfilled and decided I needed some sort of outlet for my weird ideas (because "Baby formula ads are not the time or place for characters with quirky fetishes, Kelly"). So one day I scribbled down a request for someone to dress up as a lobster and race me around my apartment and posted it as an online classified ad. I had no expectation of anything coming of it. But when people started responding to the ad, I realized I might have stumbled onto something. I kept posting newer, weirder ads, and people kept responding, and, well, here we are.

Race Me in a Lobster Suit is a collection of email

conversations I had with strangers who responded to the fake ads I posted on the internet. In each case, you'll see the original post and the full email exchange that resulted when someone replied and I tried to keep the conversation as lengthy and entertaining as possible. "Why do that, Kelly?" you might ask. Great question; I asked myself that same thing more than once along the way. Like the time I came up for air from my Google search about ways to perform an at-home exorcism.

"How do you think of this stuff?" is another question I was asked a lot as I worked on this book. p. 169 Basically, I throw a ton of ideas at the wall and see what sticks. Sometimes nothing does. In fact, a lot of the conversations went nowhere, and sometimes it took reposting the same ad a number of times before I figured out where I would take the story once someone replied. More often than I'd anticipated, I got caught off guard P. 100 because someone was *so* willing to do something I never p. 39 thought they'd do. Posing nude with a deadly animal, for example, or chasing me through Midtown Manhattan in a tarantula costume . . . that sort of stuff.

In the process I encountered seriously funny strangers, and in my attempts to seem authentic I learned weird p. 93 things. I know more about boa constrictor live births than I ever thought I would. And if you're ever in the market for tranquilizer darts or bulk orders of fresh seaweed, I can point you in the right direction. p. 13

p. 100 again But it wasn't all absurd email conversations and funny web searches. The toughest part of the project was coming clean to the strangers I'd been telling the wildest lies of my life to. When one of us finally hit a breaking point I'd confess, and I was always nervous what the reaction might be. I'm happy to say that most people were amused by the banter. However, some were . . . not amused. Those reactions ranged from silence to a mixed bag of "Go [fill in the blank]"s.

nervous laugh

I'm not sure what your takeaway from this book will be, but I'll share mine: people are funny. I can't explain why some folks entertained the idea of my ads for so long. Maybe they wanted a good story, which is an attitude I can get behind any day. Maybe they were trolling me back. Or maybe we're all just bored. Whatever the reason, I encourage you to talk to strangers. It's very fun. And I'm not talking about the white van, "do you want some candy" types of strangers, OK? Don't take my suggestion out of context. I'm talking about the strangers you meet online who are willing to come over and play dead for a fixed hourly rate. Those strangers rule.

Back to that day at the phone store: I'd recently been emailing back and forth with a guy about dressing him up like a doll and brushing his chest hair on the Great Lawn in Central Park (minor details) before confessing that I'd made the whole thing up and that I wanted to publish our conversation in a book. Before he gave me permission to do so, he insisted we speak on the phone. So to avoid sharing my real phone number, I ended up in another awkward exchange, this time with a very nosy AT&T sales guy. For the record, it didn't work out with the doll guy, and you won't find that conversation in this book.

But the same ad yielded another conversation with someone else, so look forward to reading "Tea Party" on page 157. (All the people in this book allowed me to publish their emails, but no real names have been used.)

In all seriousness, I sincerely appreciate you buying this book, especially if you're not one of my mom's friends. It's not that I don't appreciate all of my mom's friends buying this book (because I do), it's just that I don't think they had a choice. Anyway, thank you for coming with me on this strange ride. I hope you laugh. And if you don't, you can hire someone to tickle you until you do. I know a guy.

Lobster Racing

Looking for individual to participate in biweekly lobster race. The way it works is, we set up an obstacle course around my apartment in Flatbush. The first lobster to cross the finish line wins. No worries if you don't have your own lobster costume, I have a spare (size M/L). Beginners are welcome this month since I twisted my ankle, which has greatly impacted my agility.

I can be lobster #1!!! Please reply with more information. Where? When? Prize???

ME > I'm happy to tell you more about the races. Typically, it is one opponent and myself; however I have, on occasion, had people ask to bring a friend. I have one extra lobster costume if you do not have one of your own or if it is at the dry cleaners, etc. It is a size M/L, but can be belted if it is too large . . . you don't want the fabric to get in your way while you're crawling around.

Before you come over, I will dress the apartment to simulate the ocean floor to make the race as realistic as possible.

Some people like to come over earlier to help me set up the course to "level the playing field." Not a problem, just let me know. We can do one night this or next week, let me know your availabilities so I can get planning.

CAM > I can come tomorrow night, and will bring friend if that's ok. Time/address/prize??

ME › Hey, I will need a little more notice so I can dress the apartment accordingly. Maybe we can plan for one night next week? I have to order all the seaweed and clams and stuff to spread all over. I also need to move my furniture into storage for the night. Your friend is more than welcome to join us as a spectator or as a competitor. The more, the merrier. Since I only have one spare costume, I ask that one of you dresses in a head-to-toe red jumpsuit to match the other racers as closely as possible. And I think I can get my hands on an extra pair of lobster lenses.

CAM › Of course that is completely reasonable. Can you do next Tuesday? If not, just tell me when. My friend will come to spectate only.

ME › Ok great, if your friend is going to spectate, she will still need a pair of lenses to see in the pitch-black darkness. Do either of you have any allergies to seaweed or kelp of any kind? There will be a ton of it everywhere. Monday night I will dress the apartment to look exactly like the ocean floor and Tuesday we will race.

CAM › No allergies. TUESDAY!

ME › Yeah! Now I just have to find a storage unit for the night and a neutral third party to come booby trap the apartment for us.

CAM › I will train to make for the best race.

ME > You should practice slow crawling and scooting backwards by curling and uncurling your abdomen. Did you know lobsters can run at 11 mph? They are so amazing.

YOU CAN ALSO PRACTICE HIDING IN SMALL CREVICES, WHICH I WILL ALSO CREATE IN THE APARTMENT NEXT TUESDAY. IF YOU HAVE A CABINET UNDER YOUR KITCHEN OR BATHROOM SINK, THAT'S A GOOD SIZED HOLE TO TRY TO SQUEEZE INTO.

If I think of anything else you can do to prep I'll let you know.

CAM > Thank you for your advice, that's very honorable. This is my first lobster race, and I'm grateful to you for sharing your knowledge.

ME > Sometimes I tie my ankles together to really challenge myself. That's how I got so good. But it's also how I sprained my ankle.

CAM > :(So sorry to hear. When did you start racing, if you don't mind my asking?

ME > Oh, I would say I've been doing it for about a year now.

CAM > WOW. Lol. A lot of experience, it should be good race.

ME > It should.

THE FOLLOWING MORNING . . .

ME > Yup. So last night I was looking at the extra lobster costume and I realized it felt a little crusty. I guess the last person to use it was slipping and sliding around in some really wet seaweed, and the saltwater dried and left it stiff. Since my dry cleaner asked me to please stop bringing in my costumes because they "make his store smell like dead fish," I decided to wear it around my apartment to break it in and make it easier to crawl and scuttle in. Well, I ended up banging into a book case and getting a nosebleed and there is some blood down the front of the costume (kind of a lot). I just wanted to warn you so you don't get nervous. You guys probably wouldn't have even noticed it since the costume is red, but I just wanted to assure you ahead of time that the blood is mine.

CAM > Can you send a picture of the costume? I might be able to remove the stain prior to the race.

ME > It really blends right into the deep red fabric, it's just a little bit darker in this large spot. I already threw it in the bathtub to soak anyway. I just didn't want you guys to get scared by the amount of blood though in case you did notice it. I've gotten nosebleeds before, but this was a really bad one.

ME > Ok, so I'm moving all of my stuff into storage tonight! The unit comes out to about $400 for the night, not sure if you wanted to split that two or three ways since

your friend is just spectating. I'm cool with it either way. If you have Venmo, that would be the best way to send me your share. Then tomorrow morning, I'll give the apartment its ocean floor makeover and we'll be off to the races! Tomorrow night for sustenance, I was thinking sushi? Thoughts?

ME ⟩ Hey, the apartment looks incredible. I would think a lobster actually lived here if it wasn't my own apartment. It even smells exactly like the ocean. I woke up extra early and made a pit stop at Fulton Street market this morning for some fish. Definitely adds an extra touch. When can I expect you guys?

ME ⟩ Hey, are you guys on your way?

CAM > Address?

ME > Hi. You emailed me so late, I fell asleep in my lobster costume waiting up for the race. I have to get rid of all of this seaweed and fish today because it stinks from sitting out since yesterday. I also have a voicemail from my landlord. One of my neighbors complained about the odor. He let me off with a warning. I also have to go pick up all my furniture by 1 pm.

This was a lot of hard work, but I am willing to reschedule. Anything for a good race.

Private contractor needed

I'm looking for a private contractor to do some work in my apartment. I'm trying to install an indoor pool. And let's keep this off the books. The apartment below me is vacant, so I'd like to try to bang this out before the first of next month. My living room is 18 x 20, so plenty of room for a decent sized pool. Don't think a diving board is feasible, but am open to a professional opinion. Email me with a good time for you to check out my place and talk logistics.

My name is Bob, I am responding to your posting. I have many years of experience. Your request is unusual, but doable. Give me a call and let's discuss. I can be reached at xxx-xxxx.

ME > That's great news. So I'd love to give you an idea of what I'm thinking. I'd like the pool to be deep enough on one end for diving but also have a shallow end for drinking and chicken fights. Not sure what the best way to do this is, but I'll leave that to you because you're the expert. Let me know what you think.

BOB > A floor gradient from shallow to deep is standard in many pools. What is your budget for this project by the way?

ME > Well we can discuss because I have no idea what a project like this costs. Before I forget, another thought I had was to turn the smaller bedroom in the downstairs apartment into a cabana for changing and hanging out.

BOB > Can you please text or call me. When are you looking to get started on this project

ME > Ironically, my phone got waterlogged over the weekend and is out of commission at the moment but I'll be checking emails. We can start next week. I was also thinking about turning the larger bedroom downstairs into a tiki bar but we can just start with the pool for now and see what that runs me.

BOB > Well if you own both floors we can build whatever you want

ME > Love to hear that you can make all of my visions come to life. Just to confirm, we are knocking out the 23rd floor ceiling/24th floor living room floor to accommodate an in-ground pool in my 24th floor apt. We will convert the smaller of two bedrooms in the downstairs apt into a cabana/changing room for pool guests. We will convert the larger bedroom downstairs into a fully functioning tiki bar. Lastly, I actually just rent the top floor. But the bottom floor is empty—no tenants for this whole month, so we'll be fine to work in there. Let me know if I missed anything or if you have any questions/comments/concerns.

BOB >

ARE YOU SAYING THAT YOU DON'T OWN EITHER APARTMENT?

ME > That's right but the downstairs one is totally empty, trust me. I keep checking. We'd probably have to create an entryway connecting the two apartments. Maybe directly to the bedroom, since the pool will likely fill the downstairs living room. I was thinking a cool spiral staircase or a slide.

BOB > ??? you are asking me to build a pool in an apartment that's not yours? two apartments that aren't yours?

ME > No no no no no. Big misunderstanding. I'm asking you to put the pool in my apartment. Because it is in-ground, it will dip in to the apartment downstairs. We can forget all of the extra cabana and bar stuff down there if it's a problem. Let's focus on the pool.

BOB > This whole thing is a problem. Quit wasting my time.

ME > We should probably discuss how to get all of the materials and your crew (assuming this is not a one-man job) past building security. I have a doorman, but if everyone comes dressed in suits and brings a change of work clothes, I don't think they'll even look twice. They're mostly on their phones anyway.

BOB >

THIS PROJECT IS NOT FEASIBLE AND YOU ARE INSANE.

Free tattoos

I'm looking for volunteers to let me tattoo them.
Limitless freehand tats per customer unless a ton of
people are interested. Don't bring references as I
probably can't replicate them well or at all. I have very
little experience with a tattoo gun, actually none, but
I bought one off eBay and I need practice. If you're
willing to be my canvas you will be compensated with
beautiful or just okay everlasting body art.

RESPONSE FROM TONY

Hey, I'm responding to the ad on craigslist about free tats. What kind of tats are you giving? I have some room and would let someone practice... depends on what size it is though.

ME > Hey man. Really excited to put this ink gun to use. I could do any size really, I'll be freehanding it. Where were you thinking of getting a tattoo?

TONY > I have some space on my thigh that I think I could give you and people won't really see if it doesn't go well since you're learning.

But what's the free tat? Why can't I bring in a reference? I was thinking maybe a skull with flames or something cool and simple like that.

ME > Loving where your head is at. Simple is good since this is going to be the first tattoo I ever give in my life. Feel free to bring a reference, I just can't make any promises to how closely it will look like it. Honestly, I'm really pumped about this and I have some ideas myself for how to take this tat to the next level.

TONY › This is your first tattoo ever? Ok I'll keep it simple then for sure so it will be more like a prison tattoo or something. Probably a skull. But what are your ideas? Also where are you going to be doing the work?

ME › I'll be working out of my uncle's shop for now. It was awesome of him to let me use the space. A skull sounds dope. How do you feel about text? Some bold block letters could be cool. I was thinking something like "BIG SAL & SONS AUTO BODY SHOP" and then under it in smaller letters it could say something like "Locally owned and operated." Also I was thinking about a cool outline. Like of Staten Island or something like that? Just a thought.

TONY › Hahaha. That's really funny but I think I'll just stick with the skull. Maybe a skull outline would be cool though. Let's talk about it. Where's your uncle's shop, is he a tattooist too?

ME › Nah, he has an auto body shop out in Staten Island. He's letting me use his back room. Anyway, I have plenty of other ideas too. I'm just throwing things out there. Feel free to be honest. A skull outline sounds sick. I should be able to do that freehand no problem as long as I stare at a picture of a skull right before. What did you think about the idea of some lettering?

ME > Hey man, if you don't want to come into the body shop that's cool too. I can set up a corner in my apartment if you'd rather come there. Did you give the lettering any thought? I wrote down a bunch of stuff I think is cool. I can share if you want.

TONY > Oh hey sorry. I got in an argument with my wife about this but I think we worked it out. The body shop would probably be better as long as it's clean. Some lettering might be cool, I'll have to think about what it would say though. Maybe something like "ride or die" or "live before you die."

ME > Dude. I fucking love that, excuse my French. "Ride

or die" would be so perfect and it can totally relate to cars. Maybe we could put like a wrench or a wheel under it and then S&S Auto and a smaller line like "Quality craftsmanship from the #1 in Auto Repair" or something. What do you think?

TONY > fnew plan s. skull with winghs that say FO EAALGES!!! FUCKING YWAHH WE FUCKOING WIUNS!

Adn no car bullshiw

ME > Hey... Just making sure I got this straight. So now you want a skull with wings and four eagles having sex tattoo'ed onto your thigh? How much real estate are we talking about here? I'm afraid that many eagles might take up a lot of space. I'm also not confident I'll be able to draw them mating but I will try.

TONY > Sorry about that, I had too many beers during the game. I think that if we put the wings on the skull that'd be cool though, kind of like Viking or something, can you do that? Where did the eagle sex come from? I didn't mention eagle sex. Also the letters should say "ride or die" not "go eagles." Can I come in this weekend? Where's your uncle's shop.

ME > Sorry I must have misunderstood. I read that as "FOUR EAGLES FUCKING, YEAH WE FUCKING." My bad. I agree the wings coming out of the skull would be awesome. And then above it we could put "SAL &

SONS AUTO BODY SHOP, MAKING CARS FLY SINCE 1996." The skull's eyes can be little outlines of Staten Island. What do you think...

My uncle's shop is in Staten Island. Let me check with him about this weekend.

TONY › What? No why do you keep bringing up cars is this some weird car repair ad thing?

ME › So my Uncle Sal and I made a deal that he would let me "rent" the office in his auto shop to do some tattoo'ing out of it if I agreed to do some marketing for him. I thought I could just buy some ad space to promote the shop but I wound up spending all my money on a tattoo gun instead. I didn't think it through. He told me I better find a way to keep my end of the bargain or I'm out, so I figure if I tattoo an ad for the shop onto someone, that'll shut him up. Like a walking billboard. I bet everyone who sees it will want to know where you got your cool tattoo. I can still incorporate the skull and I can think of some other cool slogans if you want too.

TONY › Will I get a discount for him fixing my truck at his shop? If he will give me a good deal on fixing my car forever I'll think about it since the tattoo will be on me forever.

ME › Yeah but the tattoo is free. I'm giving you an amazing permanent piece of art. Don't you think that's enough?

TONY > No it's an ad for your uncle. And you've never tattooed before so it's not going to be good. I want my truck fixed. A mouse died in the heater vent and I can't get it out and they said it'd be 1000 dollars to fix it which is stupid. If your uncle wants an ad on me, I need to have my truck repaired for free.

ME > Dude come on, I thought you trusted me. Look my uncle isn't gonna go for this. I wasn't even gonna tell him about the tattoo until after I did it. I thought if it looked cool, he might like it. But there is NO WAY he's gonna be cool if then I tell him he has to do a $1000 repair job on your truck for free. He'd actually lose his shit and maybe kill me. I need to do this for no cost to him...or me because like I said I spent all my money.

TONY > Ha no. I'm not going to let you tattoo me with your uncle's auto repair shop for free with your bad tattoo. I bet he's bad at fixing cars anyway, otherwise why'd he let you tattoo out of it.

AND I DON'T NEED ANOTHER STATEN ISLAND TATTOO BECAUSE I'M FROM THERE AND ALREADY HAVE ONE. THIS IS DUMB. I HOPE YOUR UNCLE GETS MAD AT YOU!

ME > Look, I get you're angry about the discount but my

uncle and cousins have been in the business since 1996 and trust me they know cars, ok. If somebody wants their car fixed in Stapleton Heights, they go to Sal & Sons. That's first off. Second off, I don't know why you're on the attack. I'm trying to draw something really cool on your body for no cost at all and you want to get greedy. I said I'd do the skull you wanted, I was just throwing out some ideas to make it better and unlike any other tattoo out there. How many times have you seen the same plain old skull with wings? Probably a million. What if I sweetened the pot and throw in a few mousetraps for your truck? Will you let me do the tat then?

ME › Also can I do it on your back or chest because I went back and looked at how many letters there are and it's a lot. We're gonna need way more room.

TONY › You haven't done a tattoo before so of course it's not going to be good. You're practicing. I'm doing you the favor because I'm letting you practice and I don't want an ad for a shop on me for free. NO. And I don't need mousetraps for my truck thank you the mouse is already dead and it stinks which is why I need the repair. I also don't like being tricked. Thanks no thanks goodbye I hope your uncle gets mad at you and you learn a lesson.

Free personal training sessions

Looking for volunteers to try out my new full body workout program. This new extreme conditioning program will sculpt your muscles and your confidence in no time through high intensity interval training and protein. The program is called "Meat Your New Body," and I will be shooting workout videos around NYC in the upcoming weeks as marketing materials. Don't miss your chance to be among the first to jump onto NYC's latest fitness craze. Guaranteed there will be studios specializing in this popping up across the city over the next few months. Email me if interested and I'll send you a bit of what the program entails.

I'm willing to give some free personal training sessions to get the ball rolling. If it's ok, I'd love to document your transformation.

Hi. My name is Donnie. I would like to hear more about your workout plan.

ME ⟩ Ok, can you tell me a bit about your current workout routine? What type of exercise, how many times per week, etc. This will determine where we start and what materials we should have on hand.

DONNIE ⟩ I usually do 30 minutes on the treadmill to start and then lift weights. Mostly arms and legs. Don't really do abs or much else.

ME ⟩ Nice. The great thing about this program is that it is a series of workouts using protein at its core. I can send you a sample circuit if you'd like so you can get a feel for what I'm going for.

DONNIE ⟩ Sure. I never really got into the whole protein thing so I'd like to know what you have in mind.

ME ⟩ You got it my man. Here is a small taste of my customized workout routine. A combination of plyometrics and cardio will help you lose weight and *beef* up at the same time.

HAM BAM: In this plyometrics training exercise we explosively toss a Virginia ham back and forth for 5-8 minutes to develop strength and dynamic flexibility.

LEAN MEAT SPRINTS: In this endurance workout we wrap our lower halves in slices of lean deli cut meats like Ovengold roasted turkey to increase our body weight and then hop on the treadmill for sprints.

WEIGHTED HANGER CRUNCH: Hanger steaks are a great way to add difficulty to an exercise you've mastered. Adding a few pounds of beef to this traditional core-focused move will make all the difference.

Happy to answer any questions and to get the ball rolling. Let's talk schedules.

DONNIE > Is this a joke?

ME > No, I have spent months coming up with this program. Why?

DONNIE >
NO OFFENSE BUT WHY FOODS? I'M SURE THERE ARE OTHER THINGS YOU COULD USE INSTEAD FOR THE SAME EFFECTS WITHOUT THROWING AROUND A HAM.

ME > Sure, but this is a brand-new take on the same old boring routine, with protein quite literally at its core. Many people don't understand the importance of protein when it comes to working out. These items serve as our equipment, yes, but double as fuel. Between sets, can you take a bite out of a medicine ball? No. After sprints, can you chow down on the treadmill? I don't think so. Ever tried biting into a dumbbell? I wouldn't recommend it. But a T-bone steak or a country ham? You can take a bite and turn it into pure muscle right on the spot.

DONNIE > Yeah I don't know if it works like that.

ME > Leave it to me, I'm the expert. Look, I can customize the workout to your problem areas, fitness goals, you name it. And we're only just getting started here Donnie. Here are a few more exercises from my program that will really focus on that core of yours.

FLANK PLANKS: In this new take on the traditional plank, we will take this core-centric exercise to the next level by adding a flank steak to your back every 30 seconds as you continue to hold the position, adding weight and difficulty to really challenge your midsection.

ALBACORE POWER SLAMS: Stand with feet hip-width apart and grasp the ends of two mid-size albacore tunas by the tails. Bring both arms overheard before forcefully slamming the fish to the ground and lowering into a high squat. Straighten and repeat.

Let me know your availabilities and we can get started ASAP.

DONNIE ⟩ To be honest this sounds really crazy. Where do you plan to do these workouts? In public? And where are you getting all of these meats from?

ME ⟩ Anywhere. Parks, gyms, the Y, you name it.

MY UNCLE OWNS A BUTCHER SHOP IN THE WEST VILLAGE SO I CAN GET ALL KINDS OF MEATS. THEY JUST HAVE TO BE BACK IN THE MEAT LOCKER THE WAY WE FOUND THEM BY SUNRISE

MINUS THE BITES WE TAKE. BY
THE WAY YOU HAVE TO TAKE SMALL
NIBBLES FROM ONE SIDE OF THE
MEAT.

DONNIE > LMAO do you even know how nuts this all is?
I'll just join a gym. Good luck with your meat program.
I'll be on the lookout for people exercising with huge
pieces of meat.

ME > Come say hi if you see us.

Looking for someone to make my dreams come true

Over the last few weeks I've been having a series of recurring nightmares that I can't get to go away. My shrink chalks it up to stress. I guess that makes sense since I have so much on my mind right now. What I'm looking for is someone to come over to reenact my bad dreams with me. I keep a dream journal, so I have them all written down. I think if I fall asleep to them happening in real life, my subconscious might start doing something different once I fall asleep. I say it's at least worth a try.

Hi! My name is Drew and I'm an actor living in NY.

Your request to have someone act out your dreams with you actually sounds super interesting. Weird, but interesting. Would you be willing to do it over Skype? I'm really busy and kinda live in the middle of nowhere, so commuting would be hard for me.

Also, to be totally honest I'm not comfortable doing this with you in person right off the bat, but maybe if we get to know each other after a while?

Let me know.

ME > Hey Drew, thanks so much for emailing. My shrink thinks what will make this role-playing useful is actually acting out the scenarios. So I think you would have to be here to do it in person. If you'd like I'd be happy to tell you about the dream and how I imagine we would act it out.

DREW > I've given it some thought, and as long as my friend Vince can come and hang out we should be fine. Just at first, to make sure everything is safe. I've met some real weirdos in this city hahaha.

Anyway, tell me about your dreams. Wow, now I sound like a shrink.

BTW, how much are you offering for this again? I don't remember if I saw in the original post.

Sincerely,
Drew

ME > I guess it'd be ok for your friend Vince to join us. Honestly I've had some other recurring nightmares that he could even act out with us . . . In fact a third person would even be helpful. But for the past several weeks I've been having this one dream about a giant tarantula that I need to tackle first.

In the dream, the tarantula lowers himself from the ceiling above my bed to attack me. He is wielding eight sharp knives and once he reaches the bed, he chases me all around. It's absolutely horrifying. When do you think you and Vince would be able to come help me?

DREW > Wow, that sounds terrifying! I can understand why you'd want it to stop!

I can ask him, but Vince doesn't participate in the things I bring him along to. He's just there to make sure everything runs smoothly. Don't worry though, he's very discreet and usually stays out of sight. But as long as he comes along, I'm more than willing to help you re-enact anything you'd like! :) I do charge an extra 60 dollars an hour though when Vince is there, to cover his expenses.

But like I said, after we get to know each other a little better, we might not need him.

Let me know if that sounds good.

Sincerely,
Drew

ME > Hey Drew,

I'm so happy you guys are in. I had that dream again last night, and enough is enough. So, I was thinking you could dress up in a giant tarantula costume and lower yourself from the ceiling above my bed, just like in the dream. You should be thrashing around and waving the knives. I've been researching online and I think we can fasten some kind of rope and pulley system for you to lower yourself down with, I'll probably need some help setting that up.

As for Vince, he can stay out of sight in my bathroom, which lord knows, could use a proper scrubbing.

I HAVEN'T CLEANED MY TOILET SINCE I DREAMT THERE WAS A WITCH LIVING INSIDE OF IT. I KNOW THAT SOUNDS CRAZY, BUT THAT WAS A BAD ONE...

By the time he's done with that and the shower molding, we'll probably be finished with the knife fight and heading out on our chase... I suspect you'll want him trailing us so he can keep an eye on you, yes?

Let me know how all of that sounds and if you'd like any more details. Really appreciate you and Vince tag teaming this one.

DREW > Hey, apologies. I've been out of town.

So, a couple things. First, the short answer is yes, but under a couple conditions. When I do kink work with people, I usually set a couple ground rules beforehand, which we can go over in person. It makes sure everyone is safe, and we know what's allowed both personal boundary wise and legally, don't

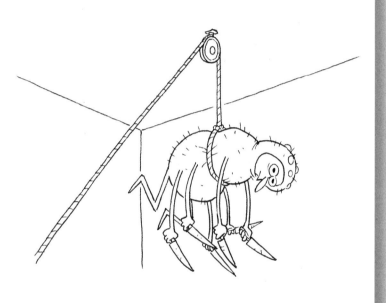

"I'VE MET SOME REAL WEIRDOS IN THIS CITY HAHAHA."

want either of us to do something that might get us in too much trouble ;)

But as far as the rigging goes, I think I'd feel safer doing that with some sort of purpose-built rig, or if you had a contractor come in and install something into a supporting structure. Years of theatre have taught me that it takes more than you think to support human weight.

Finally, what's this about a chase?

Also, you're more than welcome to ask Vince to clean... but I don't know how well that will go over.

Sincerely,
Drew

ME > Hey, a couple of things on my end as well.

THE LAST THING I WOULD CALL A HUMAN-SIZED TARANTULA TRYING TO MURDER ME WITH KNIVES IS KINKY. THIS IS NOT, LIKE, A FETISH. YOU SHOULD SEE THE LOOK IN HIS EYES AS HE CHASES ME. IT'S NOT SEXY, IT'S VERY SCARY STUFF. I'VE ACTUALLY WOKEN UP IN TEARS SO IF I FEEL UNSAFE, THEN YOU'RE DOING A GREAT JOB.

As for lowering yourself onto the bed, right now there's a large antique chandelier over my bed. If you'd prefer, you can dangle from that and drop onto the bed. I think it's pretty sturdy and I'll roll out of the way so you don't land on me. I have like ten pillows on my bed, so don't worry about getting hurt and please try not to break the bed. Since you're in theater and all that I'm sure you must know a few costume designers, right? Can you get your hands on a giant tarantula costume?

As for the chase... right after he throws the final knife at my head in the dream, the spider chases me out of the apartment and through the streets of Manhattan. The dream usually ends in an alley. I punch the tarantula square in the jaw and then lock him in a Dumpster. Again, Vince can 100% be present for this, but he cannot interfere.

Last but not least, I was just trying to make Vince's being there worth the additional $60 per hour. If he doesn't want to clean my bathroom, that's fine. I expect we'll be making quite a bit of noise with our reenactment. How is he with babies? I doubt my 2 month old is going to sleep through this.

DREW ⟩ First, I want to apologize for assuming this was a kink thing. Given the complexity of the situation, I just assumed that it was something along those lines.

That being said, I don't think this will be quite the right fit for me, especially if there are children involved.

This seems like something you should explore doing with your mental health professional.

Good luck!

ME › Drew, Vince and my husband can handle the baby. You would be dealing with me only. I'll pump beforehand so they will literally have no reason to interrupt us. Let me know if this changes your mind.

DREW › It does not.

Experienced knitter needed

I'm looking for a skilled knitter to come over and knit me into a cocoon for the rest of the winter, leaving just a small mouth hole for food and a butt flap. It's starting to get very cold out, so I won't be leaving my apartment until spring, when I emerge from my woven capsule. I do this every winter as a symbolic self-metamorphosis ever since I watched a butterfly do it at the Bronx Zoo. Knitting can be completed in a day or two, depending on your availability.

I would actually love to...

ME > Perfect. How long do you think this project will take?

LORI > Well it would depend on the thickness of the yarn, but it would probably take around 70 hours. I don't know exactly how large you are or what yarn you are using...

ME > Will you be staying with me for the duration of the job or will you be coming and going daily?

LORI > I don't think I could do it in one sitting, so yes I would be coming and going daily. I don't know how you would be planning on compensating but the narrower the time frame the more I would probably have to charge just because it would kind of be exhausting to do for more than 8 hours at a time.

ME > That's fine. You can take your time. Is there a way for me to remain in the unfinished cocoon while you are away? Once I'm inside, I don't want to come out until spring. I don't want to destroy the work in progress though if I sleep or shower in it, etc.

LORI > How will you be showering in the cocoon? I just think the wool might shrink — not that it gets too tight.

ME > I did some research and I believe soaking in hair conditioner and gently stretching the fabric can unshrink it. I'll do this each time I bathe and dry off, so twice a day until spring. Will I be able to crawl around my apartment in my cocoon the way you are imagining it?

LORI > Hello, are you still looking for someone? Damn. We spoke a few weeks ago briefly and I honestly thought it was a joke, because this is an extremely difficult thing to do... When you were talking about showering etc. I was about to say that the wool WILL shrink no matter how much conditioner you use. I would do it but I really don't know what you are expecting or how you expect to pull this off.

ME > I thought the whole conditioner thing was very clever, Lori, and I was disappointed when you didn't respond because I lost a few days in my pupa. So I want to be tightly wound into this cocoon from the outside. Is there a way to knit it around my body from the ground up (or head down) like how a caterpillar makes a cocoon around its own body. You can move in a cyclical motion around me until it is complete. Just tell me if this is possible.

LORI > It's possible, but it will be more like a crochet than a knit. It'll look the same though but that is the best way to do something so big.

ME > That's fine.

LORI > How much are you willing to spend on this because you are going to have to buy A LOT of wool and it isn't cheap and paying someone to knit for like 30 hours will also not be cheap even at an extremely low hourly rate....

ME > I'm willing to pay.

IT IS VERY IMPORTANT TO ME THAT I BE WOVEN TIGHTLY INSIDE MY CHRYSALIS ALL WINTER AND EMERGE A BEAUTIFUL BUTTERFLY COME SPRING.

Tell me will this crochet be tight around my body? I can set up a harness from the ceiling and dangle from it if this will make it easier for you to work around me. Let me know if this would be helpful.

LORI › The crochet can be tight and I think the harness would be helpful...

ME › Ok, I will install the harness from my living room ceiling and hang from my feet while you crochet. I'm thinking a third hole in addition to the two I specified in my post might be a good idea... on the side, so I can stick an arm through to do things. What do you think?

LORI › Have you hung from your feet for long periods before? It could get painful... I think the third hole is a good idea though.

ME › And the small mouth hole for breathing/eating and the butt flap are fine I'm assuming. I have only hung from my feet once before. It was to be woven into my cocoon last winter.

LORI › Do you have photos from the last time? I would love a reference.

ME › I don't have any photos, I was unable to take any of myself from inside the cocoon. I tried but they all came out really dark. And then there was an incident with Gretta (the lady who wove me into my cocoon last year) so she never took any photos of me.

LORI › An "incident"?

ME › Yeah I passed out while she was knitting me into the cocoon. She started from the bottom, so my head was

covered almost immediately so she didn't realize I was
unconscious for a while. Then she thought I was dead and
called 911, and they came... it was a whole thing. Anyway,
do you think a pair of collapsible butterfly wings would fit
inside the cocoon if I wore them on my back?

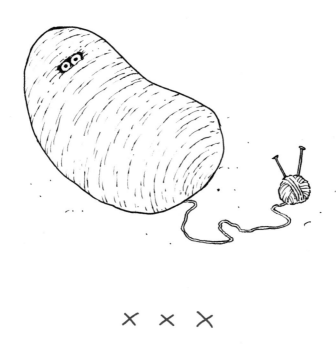

× × ×

Looking for someone to help me make a racket

For the past two years I have made it my mission to create a cacophony of monstrous proportions to confuse the living hell out of my downstairs neighbors. They're a couple of young dudes in their mid-twenties. I know they want to know what I'm doing up here because my super has mentioned it to me on multiple occasions. I'm looking for someone to join me one night this week for a few hours to make a lot of strange loud sounds through the floor. Your job will range from some light stomping to spilling bags of marbles and so on. Feel free to bring anything loud that you own.

Hi, my name is Nick and I am interested in helping you make some loud noise to screw with your downstairs neighbors.

Please let me know what you are offering and when you would like to do this, as I am available most evenings. Thank you.

ME > Hey Nick! I would love to make this happen one night this week, maybe Thursday or Friday? Do you have any loud objects you could bring over?

NICK > Either of those nights works for me. And I have a lot of loud things. Anything specific you're looking for?

ME > You wouldn't happen to have a vacuum, would you?

NICK > Actually, I do have a vacuum.

ME > That's awesome! Can you bring it?

NICK > Yes I can. Do you know what time you would want to do this?

ME > Great. My apartment could really use a once over. Let's shoot for Thursday! Anything else you could bring? Do you have a sledgehammer? I'm about to remodel my kitchen and need to tear out some cabinets.

NICK > Not a sledgehammer but a few hammers that could do the trick. I also walk with a heavy cane sometimes, I may need to bring that. And Thursday sounds great.

ME > Let's shelf the hammers for now—you're not gonna believe this but I was able to get my hands on a pipe organ... you know like they play in churches?? Actually a church uptown was getting rid of an old one. The thing is so gigantic and so so loud. I need to scoop it up in the next day or two but my work schedule is nuts. Any way you think you'd be able to swing that? I can leave a spare set of keys to my apt for you at the Starbucks nearby. You can leave it basically anywhere in my living room.

NICK > I could prob get it tomorrow afternoon or Wednesday.

ME > That is perfect.
And the good news is the
church isn't too far from
my apartment so I really

don't think you'd even need to rent a U-haul. You could probably just wheel it a few blocks and then use the freight elevator at my place. I can let Pastor Anthony know you're coming.

ME ⟩ If you're available tomorrow, you can pick up the organ—I spoke with someone at the church. You might have to transport the pipes in pieces, but I think you can wheel the base to my apartment. I'll leave you a key, feel free to help yourself to anything in the fridge.

NICK ⟩ Yea, I can pick it up tomorrow. I can let you know in the morning what time would be best for me.

ME ⟩ Thanks, man.

SO PASTOR ANTHONY ASKED IF IN EXCHANGE FOR THE ORGAN, SOMEONE WOULD BE ABLE TO ACT AS AN ALTAR SERVER IN HIS 12 O'CLOCK MASS TOMORROW. I SAID YES. LET ME KNOW IF THAT WORKS. AFTER MASS YOU CAN START BREAKING DOWN THE ORGAN.

What I didn't account for was the length of the largest pipe, which is 32 feet. I'll have to figure something out because my ceilings are not that high but let's get it all into my apartment and then we can figure out if we can make a racket with just the smaller pipes. It doesn't have to sound good, just has to be loud.

ME > I forgot to ask, are you Catholic? I don't think it matters to deliver the Eucharist to the altar to be honest.

ME > Hey Nick, I never heard back. Are you able to make mass at noon? Also, would you mind bringing the vacuum for later?

Thanks dude!

NICK > Sorry, I can't make the mass at noon. I ended up working until 4 am at my friend's bar. I can come out later to drop off the vacuum if needed.

ME > Great, when you get to my apartment if you could just vacuum the living room and bedrooms if you get there first, that would be awesome. And if you're coming from downtown would you mind swinging by Equinox and picking up my tap shoes from my locker? I can give you the combo.

NICK > When do you want me to show up?

ME > Is 1 AM too late? These young guys usually go out on Wednesday nights. Completely forgot. Is it cool if you grab my tappies?

NICK > Sure. So you want me to come out around 1 am tonight? I'll bring the vacuum and grab your taps on the way over.

"I WAS REALLY EXPECTING TO JAM
ON THE PIPE ORGAN TONIGHT."

ME > Is the organ already at my place?! Nick man, you move fast!

NICK > No it's not. I thought we couldn't get it because I wasn't able to be at the mass today.

ME > Oh my god, total miscommunication on my end. You still could have gone to pick it up later in the day. I have to give the pastor a call, I'm pretty sure he was waiting for you. I was really expecting to jam on the pipe organ tonight and really get those guys scratching their heads. I think we should reschedule until we can get it to my apartment. Thanks man.

NICK > I can move it tomorrow if you would like

ME > Ok let's do tomorrow.

I THINK YOU COULD PROBABLY MOVE THE ENTIRE THING IN ABOUT TEN OR SO TRIPS. AND MY APARTMENT IS ONLY ONE MILE FROM THE CHURCH SO IF YOU HAVE ALL DAY TO DO IT THAT'D BE PERFECT!

NICK > Ok tomorrow it is.

ME > Hey Nick, sorry. This week was REALLY crazy. I had the organ delivered, it just seemed easier that way. Let's plan a night next week. Do you have any way to get your hands on a drum set? I think with me tickling the ivories and you slamming down on some percussion, we can really give these guys a show. Also, where are we with the tap shoes?

ME > Just checking in, how are we looking for this week? I was practicing last night on the organ and one of the guys downstairs started hitting the ceiling with a broomstick. Hilarious!!!! We need to get those drums in here ASAP.

ME > Haven't heard from you in a few days. Swung by the gym today for my taps and they weren't there. Did you end up getting them??

ME > Nick? The taps!?

Need a good laugh

It's been a really long time since I had a good laugh, so I'm looking for someone to come over to my apartment and tickle me for a while. Nothing weird, just good tickle fun. I could just really use a genuine laugh to take my mind off of things.

Hey,

My name's Bill, and I'm a tickler.
I specialize in rougher, fetishistic
tickling that produces belly laughter,
but I can also do a gentler tickle
if that's what you desire. Please let
me know.

ME > Hey man, for the record this is not a fetish, although
a deep belly laugh sounds great right about now. Work has
been tough lately and I'm just looking to blow off some
steam and laugh really really hard.

BILL > Gotcha, where are you located and how much are
you willing to pay?

ME > Located downtown. Can totally discuss pay. First
let's talk logistics. I'm thinking you could go for the neck,
armpits, and belly... Also, if you squeeze right above my
knee, I will go completely insane laughing.

I ALSO HAVE THIS WEIRD NERVE IN MY BACK THAT HURTS AND TICKLES AT THE SAME TIME IF YOU HIT IT A CERTAIN WAY WHICH I SORT OF WEIRDLY ENJOY...

And then of course there's the bottom of the feet, let me tell you right now, I will be screaming at the top of my lungs laughing if you go for the feet—but totally get if you're not a foot person.

BILL ⟩ That all works for me, now I usually just use my bare hands, that works for you?

ME ⟩ Oh absolutely but if you want to tickle my feet with a large feather that also works. My lord, does that tickle.

BILL ⟩ Well, all of my things are in storage, but if I can scoop something up on my way, I'll keep that in mind. Do you want my number to make this easier?

ME ⟩ Unfortunately my wife took my phone away with her for the weekend so we will have to just email. No worries, I check my email a lot.

BILL ⟩ Okay, just wanted to make sure whatever would be more convenient for you.

ME > So what are you thinking in terms of compensation for tickle time? I'll run something by the boss (my wife handles the finances) this afternoon.

BILL > What's your budget?

ME > Ok so I called my wife and after a long "discussion" it turns out that she is not willing to entertain this. She hung up on me and now she's in a mood. Here's what I can do... I have a gift card to Bamonte's in Brooklyn... Best clams casino I have ever had, hands down. You can have it. And we'll need to talk scheduling around when she's not home. I can see a lot of laughing turning into crying if she's around.

ME > Hey Bill, have you given any thought to Bamonte's? I am telling you, those clams on a half shell are to die for. I've had a pretty rough week at work and a tickle is sounding really good right about now.

BILL > Sorry, not at the moment. However delectable the clams may be, I can't pay the landlord in half-shells. Maybe some other time.

ME > Ok that's good because I talked to the Mrs. again and Bamonte's is off the table. Apparently my mother-in-law gave us that gift certificate so she wasn't happy that I offered it up. She also, it appears, hid my checkbook. She hates that I'm doing this and clearly doesn't want me to be happy. Listen, we went to Mexico a few months ago and I'm pretty sure I have some pesos hidden in a suitcase somewhere. I can try to find those for you. How does that sound? By the way don't mention the pesos to my wife if you meet her, she doesn't know about them.

BILL > How many pesos are we talking about? Because I'll have to look up the exchange rate.

ME > Ok, I was rummaging around in my closet and my wife caught me. She took the pesos. She is being so controlling. All because she doesn't want me to pay for tickles. But will she tickle me herself? No. Would you consider tickling me like crazy in exchange for a round of beers...

ME > I take it from your lack of response that you don't drink. That's cool. I'm still looking for my checkbook. There are only so many places my wife could have hid it. But in the meantime, she is heading home to her mom's early for the holidays so I will have the apartment to enjoy to myself for a couple of days. And Bill... there is one thing she forgot to hide: the Bamonte's gift card. The certificate is stuck to our fridge and it can be yours for a small price of tickling me half to death.

BILL ⟩ I mean, normally I wouldn't take a round of beers off the table, but right now I want money.

ME ⟩ Ok, let me know if you change your mind about the clams.

Animal sound impersonator needed

Looking for someone who can do animal impressions. I'm watching my friend's pet shop for the next two weeks while he's away. In your email, please call out which animal(s) you can best mimic of the following: African gray parrot, canary, chinchilla, guinea pig, frog, fish tank filter (constant gurgling), a mixture of rodents. Please consider all sounds they make, including fluttering and scampering around their enclosures. Serious inquiries only please, I'm on a time crunch.

Hey!

I'm super confused about what you need. I'm very good at animal sounds, but I just need to understand what you're asking for.

My voice has been featured in dozens of animal movies.

Best wishes,
Matt

ME > Hey Matt, this is a huge relief. I'll explain, but can you specify which animal sounds you can make? Would be super helpful. Thx.

MATT > Alright, going off of your list:

AFRICAN GRAY PARROT - these birds are great talkers, very loud calls. No problem.

CANARY - song birds, got it. Also very sensitive to air quality.

CHINCHILLA - I did some quick research for these, not too complicated, like a guinea pig but more personality.

GUINEA PIG - my parents bred several kinds of guinea pigs, this was my bread and butter when I was just starting out.

FROG - I'm less comfortable with amphibians, but if you give me some direction we should be OK. (I'll start researching right away)

FISH TANK FILTER (CONSTANT GURGLING) - I've never impersonated a machine, what did you have in mind?

A MIXTURE OF RODENTS - very experienced; have you seen *Ratatouille*?

SCAMPERING AND CAGE SOUNDS - This may be outside my skill set. But I know a guy.

Since I'm a union actor, I need to know what kind of gig this is. I've worked with animals. I do live performances, birthdays, private sessions, etc., but if this is being recorded, I need to know in advance. Let's talk.

ME > Ok here's the situation. I'm watching a friend's pet shop for the next couple of weeks and like a jackass locked myself out. My friend is calling the shop every few days to check in on me and the animals.

IF HE HEARS SILENCE IN THE
BACKGROUND HE'S GONNA KNOW
SOMETHING'S UP BECAUSE THERE'S
USUALLY A BUNCH OF NOISE IN
THE SHOP. I NEED SOMEONE OR A
FEW PEOPLE TO COME OVER AND
MAKE SOME ANIMAL NOISES IN THE
BACKGROUND OF THE CALLS SO HE
THINKS I'M THERE.

I could record the sounds or we could just have you come in during each scheduled call to do this live. There's usually a two hour window. Live seems better to me so we can switch up the sounds each time, I can even make you some lunch if you want. The scampering guy too, if you could let him know. That'd be great.

MATT > Hey man, so I thought this through. What a crazy situation! I'd love to help but I just don't think I could do a convincing enough job to pull this off. It would take a few people and even then, your friend probably knows these sounds like the back of his hand.

I reached out to my sound editor friend who does this kind of stuff for a living. He said he could put together a few minutes of sound effects to play back during your phone call. Do you have any money to spare for this? Sounds like he would do it for $100.

MATT > Or for that price you could get a locksmith and maybe save the animals.

ME > The animals will be fine, I seriously over-fed them the other night. If not, they can be replaced later in the week. But I need to buy time here. Is this sound editor guy the one who makes the scampering noises you mentioned? If so I owe you big time because no one else has been able to make those noises at all. Still need fish tank and amphibian sounds. Let me know if you have another friend. The next time I expect a call from my buddy is this Saturday. Can you fellas lend me your talents then?

MATT > So the sound editor can use sound effects to do everything you need. It'll be a sound file you can play off your phone or some speakers, and that will sound exactly like a pet shop. I think that's your best option. Do you have money for that?

ME > For sure. So what does he need to record all your sound effects? Do I have to rent a microphone or something? Just tell me what to get. You guys can come over as early as you need to record all the sounds and combine them or whatever. I know you have a lot to cover. I can get some bagels if you guys want too. Thanks man.

MATT > I think the idea is he would do it all on his computer and just send you the file. Some amazing things he can do with sound effects.

ME > Oh ok, so you'll record it right into my computer then. Cool. Just so you know, one of the African gray parrots knows how to talk. Some kid taught him to swear so he curses up a storm sometimes. You should incorporate that into your parrot impression.

MATT > I don't think you're understanding. This guy has thousands of sound effects of animals already on his computer. He can put them together to sound like a pet shop. That way all you need to do is press "play" during your phone call, and it will sound like a real pet shop.

I'm a good actor, but I can't make three different sounds at the same time. Also I'm really worried about these animals...

Basically, I don't think we need to be there in person, is what I'm saying.

ME > Forget about the animals. I'm the one you should be worried about—I'm in deep.

Plus I dumped so much food in all their cages before I left the other night, they'll be fine for at least a few more days. I think I get what you're saying about playing the sound effects now. I didn't realize you already recorded them on his computer. You're two steps ahead of me man! Can you send me what you did so I can have a listen?

MATT > Ha, we didn't record them. These are real animal sounds that he already has. I can send over a sample later. If you like it, you can arrange to pay him.

ME > I don't understand. Where did you find the animals? When did you do all of this???

MATT > My friend is a sound editor. That means he has thousands of sound effects on his computer for work, including animal sounds. So I'm asking him to put together a sample for you. It might take a few hours.

ME > Yes, I get it. I'm not an idiot. But WHERE did he find all these animals to record on his computer? Maybe I'm not asking this clearly. Can you ask him if he has two gerbils fighting?

MATT > He went to Africa to record lions. He went to the ocean to record fish.

I DON'T KNOW MAN, WHY DO YOU NEED TWO GERBILS FIGHTING? CAN'T YOU JUST HAVE NORMAL SOUNDS? YOU NEVER MENTIONED GERBILS IN THE ORIGINAL JOB POST.

ME > I said a bunch of rodents, man. These two gerbils in there, they are always going at it. It would be so believable if when my friend calls, I can be like "Hang on man, those two gerbils are fighting again, you know the ones.

"HANG ON MAN, THOSE TWO GERBILS ARE FIGHTING AGAIN."

Let me go break this up," and then he hears the gerbils fighting in the distance and me breaking it up.

MATT > Oh sorry man you're right, I forgot. I'll ask if he can do gerbils.

ME > I've been thinking about this and I think I'd just feel better doing it live. We'd have more control. Besides, how am I supposed to play a recording on my phone if I'm using it for the phone call?

MATT > I'm just not convinced that one or two people can sound like an entire pet shop.

You could play the sounds off a laptop?

ME > Don't have one. Look, if you bring the sound editor, the scamper sound guy, and yourself that's three. And you're such a good actor you can probably switch really fast from parrot to frog to chinchilla etc. Just a few seconds of each: squawk holy shit fuck—ribbit ribbit—squeak squeak. Like that.

MATT > A real actor wouldn't turn this down. I never give up. But the sound editor is terrible at that kind of stuff. He's only a yellow belt with sound effects. I guess I could bring my kids? They make weird noises all the time (hint hint gerbils).

Do you have any friends (female/attractive/good at cooking) that could help us?

ME > I see... I should set you up with my sister...

MATT > Can I get her headshot? Also how'd the phone call go?

ME > The last time I sent her photo to a stranger she got very angry with me. But you'd get along great, being two single parents and all. She's also good at squawking... different kind of squawking. Phone call went fine. Turns out there was a small explosion in the shop and the fire department had to break in. A true blessing in disguise.

Out of loop Mom desperate to learn secret language

I'm the mother of three teenagers and recently they've been speaking this language at home that I can't understand. I've come to learn it's pig latin. Every night at the dinner table they talk to each other and I have no idea what is going on. I think they're using it as code to talk about sex, drugs, and beer. I need someone to give me some lessons in this language. I jotted down something I overheard them say last night below. Maybe you can translate it to prove you can understand it and then we can schedule a lesson.

"isthay eatloafmay astastay ikalay itshay"

Hi,

My name is Meg, I'm responding to the ad you posted. One question.

Did you have meatloaf for dinner last night?

ME > Hello, thank you for responding. Yes we did have meatloaf for dinner last night! It's their absolute favorite meal that I cook. How did you know that exactly?

MEG > That's what I thought... I hate to be the bearer of bad news but what your kids said was "This meatloaf tastes like shit." They were speaking in pig latin.

ME > Well, that can't be right. They practically lick their plates clean when I make this meatloaf. I leave the room for one minute and it's gone.

MEG > Haha I'm so sorry, but that's definitely what they said. It's pig latin. I can teach you how to speak it, it's actually very simple once you know how.

ME > Why would they say that Meg.

MEG > I don't know... maybe they're scared to tell you. A lot of people don't like meatloaf. Especially kids.

ME > So they'll say it to each other in a secret language right under my nose? What else are they talking about right in front of me that I don't know about!??

MEG > Who knows. They're teens. And a lot of people don't love meatloaf. I'm not a huge fan of it myself, admittedly.

ME > If you ate one bite of mine you would probably beg for seconds. Also, I use catsup on my meatloaf, which teens love.

MEG > Haha maybe. I think a lot of people use ketchup though? Do you still want to learn pig latin or talk about meatloaf recipes all day? Lol.

ME > Yes I do. You're almost as fresh as my kids are with that mouth. Lucky for you I'm not your mother.

MEG > Haha. I don't mean to be!

ME > Hm. So how do my kids all know this pig latin? Where does one learn to speak it?

MEG > Well it's a made up language. It's been around for a long time, a lot of kids speak it for fun or to prevent adults or non speakers from understanding what they're saying... as you know. Like I said I can teach you.

ME > Ok well are you sure you know how to speak it correctly then? Maybe they were saying this meatloaf is so delicious and you misinterpreted.

MEG > I am 100% sure that I translated it correctly. I can teach you. Are you offering any sort of compensation?

ME > Well why don't we try another so I can see if you really know how to speak it. I wrote down a few things I heard them say this week. What does this mean?

"iyay oundfay ickorlay inyay ommaysay edicinemay abinetcay"

MEG > I found liquor in mom's medicine cabinet.

ME > Oh my god.

MEG > I wouldn't get too worried. Maybe just sit them down and have a talk. I'll teach you how to translate so they won't be able to do this in front of you anymore.

ME > What does this mean:

"ichwhay oneyay ofyay om'smay oyfriendsbay eptslay overyay astlay ightnay"

MEG >

WHICH ONE OF MOM'S BOYFRIENDS SLEPT OVER LAST NIGHT...

Are they really saying these things? Why don't I just teach you so you understand what they're saying and I don't have to keep translating. That is what the ad posting was for, right?

ME > What about this one. Please.

"iyay oundfay ayay egnancypray esttay inyay ethay arbagegay"

MEG > Just take the first letter of each word, move it to the end, and add "ay," that is it.

Assistance eating burritos

I recently broke most of the bones in my body and am in a full body cast. I'm not looking for sympathy, it's all good—I moved back in with my mom and she's taking great care of me. But there's one thing she won't do. She thinks I eat too many burritos... I don't care, I love burritos and I'm gonna find a way to eat them. I can have the burrito delivered, but I have no way of eating it by myself. I need someone to come feed it to me through the mouth hole of my cast every day for the next few months. Email me if you're interested, it's been four days since my last burrito and I'm jonesing for one.

Hi, my name is Joe. I am available to help.

ME > Thanks man. I love my mom and all but she is killing me. She's been making me eat healthy when all I want is a goddamn burrito. I can't move at all, I'm just lying in bed, at least let me eat what I want. I ordered one for lunch today and it literally just sat in the kitchen. I could smell it from my bed. She basically force fed me a vegetable smoothie instead. It was disgusting.

JOE > No problem. When do you need me? How long and how much?

ME > I could probably use you this week and as long as I'm in this cast, which could be weeks or months. The only thing is I have to figure out what the best time of day is. Has to be when my mom is out or distracted enough that you can sneak in and feed me without her knowing.

JOE > I'm too old for this. Just stop eating burritos.

ME > Um, easy for you to say. You're not the one stuck in a full body cast at your mom's house on a liquid diet against his own will.

ME > Look, I know you don't want to help me, but I'm desperate. I tried ordering another burrito for dinner tonight. I even gave specific instructions to the delivery guy to walk right into the house and find me with the burrito already unwrapped for faster entry into my mouth, and of course my mother intercepted it in the living room... Not before the mouthwatering smell of hot pork and beans reached my nostrils. It was honestly torture. I need help ASAP.

JOE >

SORRY TO HEAR THAT MAN. YOU NEED TO COME TO A COMPROMISE WITH YOUR MOTHER. SNEAKING INSIDE OF YOUR HOUSE TO FEED YOU IS NOT THE BEST APPROACH.

ME > But I'm inviting you man. It's fine. Look, I think she's driving to Woodbury Commons some time in the next few days to do some shopping so that should be an all day affair. I ordered a breakfast burrito this morning because, well, I'm not a quitter and she fed it to our dog dude.

ME > Ok, so my mom will be out shopping for the whole day tomorrow. You can just slip right in with a burrito

or I can order one and you can meet the delivery guy at the door, whichever you choose, and then bring it to me in bed. When you get here, we can figure out the best technique to keep the burrito from falling apart as you feed it to me. I'm sort of lying at a weird angle and as you know, they can get very messy and fall apart if you don't hold them correctly. We need to be careful not to make a mess. If my mom comes home and finds rice and beans everywhere, the jig will be up.

ME > Hey, me again. I have a backup plan. Would you mind bringing a bag of tortilla chips with you when you come? I think our best bet to not make a mess is to line my stomach with a layer of chips to catch any falling burrito bits. Then when we're done with the burrito, we'll have nachos, and those might even be easier to feed me.

JOE > Your mom can come home unexpectedly saying she forgot something or a neighbor can see me coming in your house. If the police get called I will get locked up. I'm 39 years old. Too old for that man.

ME > It's easy man. Obviously I haven't made it to an ATM recently, but I have a checkbook. Just put the pen in my mouth, same as the burrito and I'll write you a check.

And if the police get called I'll talk to them. I'm very persuasive in my current state, people feel so sorry for me they don't even know what to do.

JOE > How much are you offering bro?

ME > Well what do you think is fair?

JOE > I really don't want to do something like this man honestly. As I said, I am 39 years old. This is something for a friend or a buddy of yours. If I do it, it has to be worthwhile. Like $150.00.

ME > Fine, ok. Do you know how to pick a lock?

Help finding ants

I knocked over my son's ant farm. He's very attached to these ants so I need someone to come help me find them all and put them back into the farm. They're running around everywhere. I wouldn't let my son take the farm with him to his dad's this weekend and now I've spilled them all over. He is going to kill me. I need to do this before he gets home tonight.

It's a waste of money to pay someone for this, sadly this is a game of time. Put something sweet in the middle of the room on top of a paper and wait... You will get the majority of the ants to come. It has to be easily accessible.

ME > Ok I will try that . . .

15 MINUTES LATER . . .

ME > Something horrible happened... I stuck my hand in a jar of jelly to smear on the wall in my son's room and when I tried to pull it out it got stuck. I kept pulling and I got it out but the jar went flying and broke and there is jelly EVERYWHERE. the couch, the floor, the carpets, the walls, THE CEILING.

THE ANTS ARE GOING INSANE.

TINA > Damn man...I guess I should have given more explicit instructions. I feel bad for you seriously... all that extra cleaning—I mean I hope something good comes of it.

ME > MY SON IS GOING TO BE HOME IN AN HOUR AND I JUST TRIPPED AND STEPPED ON LIKE 40 ANTS.

TINA > You might just have to make the trip to the store man...shit is not looking up... I mean 40/200 is nothing, think he will notice?

ME > I don't know. I'm trying to lure them back into one spot, and they're scrambling everywhere.

ME > So, I was trying to clean up the jelly and I spilled a bowl of water and I think I drowned some more... like a lot more. I don't even know how many ants I've killed at this point, but he WILL notice. The ant farm was a gift from his dad. He's going to think I did this on purpose.

TINA > Damn.... damn!!!! You gotta replace that shit! Take it easy though, keep a cool head.

ME > You're right, I need to get my chakras aligned. I'm going to put on headphones and play some meditative music while I vacuum up the dead ants. I need to hide the evidence and then I will get back to the live ones once I'm done.

10 MINUTES LATER . . .

ME > shit shit shit shit shit shit shit

TINA > What happened?

ME > It's really bad.

TINA > ???

ME > Hi. So I'm on my third glass of wine. Not only did I vacuum up about a hundred more ants, who even knows at this point, but right before I go to unplug it I hear this

loud, 'vwoop' sound, right? Turn around and realize the vacuum hose is plugged up with something so it's making this crazy noise. I pull it out of the wall and take out the bag and open it. Most of the ants are dead. I'm able to find maybe ten live ones. So I go back into my son's room to put them into the farm. What do I see? His gerbil's cage is knocked over....

TINA > Wow gotta replace that mother fucker too!!!! Damn, I honestly feel for you...

Why don't you make the story like the gerbil got out and by the time you realized it, you saw the ants everywhere and you began to panic... one hell of a Friday night...

ME > One hell of a Friday night.

Snake fashion show help

I'm having a fashion show for my pet snakes and I'm looking for some backstage help. All snakes will be modeling my own toeless sock designs. I make them into gorgeous little outfits. I'll need wardrobe assistants to help with quick changes as well as wranglers for the models. Email if interested.

Hello,

I'm replying to your ad on Craigslist because for starters, it sounds awesome. I've always been good with animals.

I've snake-sat before, so I can handle snakes fairly well. At my old job (nightclub) two of my coworkers had pet snakes. They actually brought them to the club to party with them, like props. No, they never got harmed, I made sure.

ME ⟩ Wow, that sounds very cool. I tried bringing snakes into a club once and almost got arrested. It is great to know you've handled snakes before though. This should be a cinch. Do you have any fashion experience?

ELLEN > I can sew a little bit if that's what you mean. I do have a good eye for making things match. My old boss told me the only reason he hired me was because I'm stylish. I'm not trendy stylish, more like I find my own thing and go with it.

ME > That sounds great. I need someone with an eye for fashion since there are so many outfits and quick changes. Many of the outfits have accessories, so you need to know what looks chic. Each snake has about four to five outfit changes. By the fifth, they tend to get a little irritable. You'll be wrangling them at the same time, so your keen fashion sense should help you despite all the angry snake distractions.

ELLEN > Great! All this sounds doable. How many snakes and how big are they?

ME >

THERE ARE 42 RIGHT NOW, BUT FOUR OF THEM ARE PREGNANT.

Mostly pythons and boas but a few smaller snakes as well. Sometimes some of the non-constrictors try to eat each other, so you have to make sure they all behave. I especially don't want them to eat each other backstage in their costumes. Not sure snakes can digest sequins.

ELLEN > I see, I see. That's a decent amount. Somehow I'm not surprised about the whole trying to eat each other.

Will the snakes be in tanks/cages/tables or just roaming round? Will each model be designated a certain amount of snakes to change their outfits and watch over?

ME > Well, the snakes are the models so I'm not sure what you mean.

ELLEN > I see your point, I apologize. I'm a model, so I thought you were hiring models to assist with the snakes throughout the event. My wording was wrong.

ME > That's ok. The snakes will be slithering down the runway in their getups alone. You just have to get them there. And to answer your earlier question, I usually just let them roam around. I could maybe hire another person,

but if you can handle the job alone, that would be best. Maybe a headset or clipboard would help?

ELLEN > I've only handled at most, five snakes at a time. I wouldn't be able to handle all of them on my own. Yes, a clipboard would helpful, thanks.

ME > Ok, the clipboard is no problem, although I'd probably want to have both my hands free for snake wrangling and costume changing myself. Are you comfortable tying little bonnets onto their heads and scarves around their necks as well? Some people are afraid.

ELLEN > I'm totally okay with that, not afraid of snakes. I love them. Also I have a good idea of how to hold them too. What else should I know?

ME >

HAVE YOU EVER DRESSED UP A SNAKE IN A LITTLE OUTFIT? I WILL NEED YOU TO BE ABLE TO GET THEM DRESSED AND UNDRESSED IN THEIR ENSEMBLES PRETTY QUICKLY.

While most of the outfits are thick and durable because they're made from tube socks, others are very delicate and need to be handled with care since they are made from cut-up pantyhose.

ELLEN > No, I've never dressed up a snake because my coworkers didn't dress up their snakes. If you would like to have a practice session to see how I would do, we can do so if there's time.

ME > A great way to practice leading up to the big event would be to go buy some thick rubber hosing from your local hardware store and some socks and pantyhose in various sizes. Cut the toes off the socks and just practice gliding the remaining tubes onto the hoses, being very careful as if they are live snakes in intricate sequined costumes. Another little secret is that I use the little cut-off toes to make accessories like tiny berets, scarves, and kerchiefs that you can fasten on their heads and necks.

ELLEN > That sounds solid. I might just try that. When is the event?

ME > In a few weeks. And guess what!

MY ANACONDA HAD BABIES TODAY. 58 OF THEM!

I haven't found anyone else to work the event with you so as of now you will be handling all of them yourself. But many of them are babies so don't worry. I'll be spending the next couple of weeks creating tiny runway outfits for these tiny additions.

ELLEN > CONGRATS! What a feat! But you will find other people to help me, right? I have experience with snakes, but that's a lot for me.

ME > Insane! Python babies hatched today! 74 more snakes!!!! It is a packed house over here. Maybe I can hire one other person to help you but not really sure. There are tons of babies so they will be a cinch to look after.

ELLEN > That's crazy!!! Whoa!!! Please try to get another person to help me. Maybe one of my former coworkers who's super beautiful and stylish and good with reptiles and snakes. I can ask her if she would be interested in working this event.

ME > Again, the snakes are the only models so your friend's beauty and style are irrelevant. I think you can handle this alone, Ellen.

ELLEN > I will not be able to handle that many snakes alone.

Looking for a nude model to bring to art club (male or female)

I am looking for a young and spritely nude model to come pose for my art "club." Nothing sketchy. Ha, get it? A group of friends and I have recently taken up sketching. Usually we draw bowls of fruit or city-scapes, but this week decided to take it up a notch.

Must be fairly flexible and willing to pose with live reptiles. Minimal body hair please. We artists are very meticulous about shadowing. Please describe any moles/scars/deformities. Serious inquiries only.

Hello!

I am a 20 year old man living near NYC, and I would love to pose nude for you. I am comfortable with reptiles and just shaved all my body hair (Except legs/arms. Chest/abs/pubes are clean shaved.) When and where are you hoping to have this? What is the pay?

I hope to hear back from you soon!

ME > Hi Jon, nice to meet you. You sound like you'd make a great practically hairless nude model. Tell me, have you worked with live animals before?

JON > Thank you! I haven't done a photo shoot with live animals, but I have handled animals extensively in my private life.

ME > I am so glad to hear that you are an animal lover. That makes me feel more comfortable about putting you into an enclosure with these reptiles. All of us art club members are really excited about this session as none of us have ever drawn anything like this before.

JON > Fantastic! So what kinds of animals, and how many? This sounds fun!

So talk me through the session. Also, what is pay like?

ME > Yes it does!

YOU'LL BE POSING WITH TWO ADULT MALE KOMODO DRAGONS. THEY WILL BE CONFINED IN A LARGE CAGE SO THEY DON'T MOVE AROUND TOO MUCH SINCE WE'RE TRYING TO DRAW THEM AND SINCE THEY'VE BEEN TRYING TO EAT THIS GUY PETE'S DOG ALL WEEK.

Pete is the guy whose apartment we'll be meeting at. When you come over, we'll put you inside the cage with them and we'll call out some poses to you and see how you all do. If they don't cooperate at first, no worries... we're prepared for that. We can do an hourly rate for pay. Will depend how long it takes us all to finish drawing you.

JON > Sounds good to me! Sounds fun. What's the hourly rate?

ME > Well I haven't actually hired a live model before so I'm not sure. You'll be locked in this cage with two humongous lizards for a couple of hours and I think the rate would definitely depend on how creatively involved you're willing to get. What poses are you willing to try? Is wrestling on or off the table? Will you let us strap a slab of raw meat to your body if it makes the lizards do something really interesting for us to draw?

JON > Wrestling a Komodo is highly dangerous. Even being in the same space as them is dangerous—they have been known to attack and kill humans. Raw meat is a large no-go. Again, large dangerous lizard that kills humans. Being nude with a Komodo dragon in and of itself should call for a decently high pay rate if I'm going to be honest. Are there any safety precautions? How did you even get Komodo dragons, I thought you wanted snakes?

ME > Pete is watching them for a friend who's out of town picking up some exotic bird he just bought on the black market. A few of us have pet snakes but once Pete told us about the Komodo dragons we were like, screw the snakes. If you're a real snake guy, we can maybe bring one or two of them for you to wear around your neck. To be honest, the lizards might try to eat the snakes. I don't know a ton about Komodo dragons.

Regarding safety precautions, it sort of seems like the raw meat would be a good idea. They'd probably prefer a steak over you, don't you think? We can also have a safe word. When you say it we'll unlock the cage from the outside and let you out and you can 100% say it at any point.

Again, I'm unsure about the rate since it sounds like you're not willing to do a lot of the really cool stuff. What poses do you propose? We of course want to hear what you're thinking. Then let's take it from there.

JON ⟩ Make sure they're well fed. I'm willing to pose nude with them but it's just stupid and highly dangerous to wrestle them or taunt them with food. Putting raw meat in there will just make them hungry and will entice them to attack. I'm not trying to get injured or killed. I know a decent amount about Komodo dragons - they are NOT friendly creatures and are highly illegal to own because they're so dangerous. They eat deer as a large part of their natural diet. I have no intention of touching or getting too close to either of them, again, because they're super dangerous. Even being in the cage with them is pushing limits.

You're the artist hiring a model. Make your offer.

ME ⟩ Yeah, one of them really wants to eat Pete's Great Dane... Pete says he's been pressed up against the cage licking his chops for three days. Look, I don't want you to taunt them, I want you to feed them. They'll love you after like three or four steaks. I know I would.

JON > Make an offer.

ALSO, PLEASE SEDATE THEM IN SOME FASHION. AND FEED THEM. IF THEY'RE SNAPPING AT GREAT DANES THEN THEY'LL FOR SURE EAT ME.

ME > Will you wrestle them if they are sedated and fed....

JON > Perhaps, yes. If they're fully sedated and asleep then I'll touch them and faux "wrestle."

ME > Oh, I was just gonna crush up some Benadryl to make them drowsy. They'll probably still be mostly awake. Would it help if we put Pete's dog right outside the cage as a distraction?

JON > Again, enticing with food will instigate them. The dog is food. I am food. If you're going to use exotic pets, get the proper handling. If you have a strong sedative and the right price I'm in.

Again, what is your offer?

ME > Look, I'm going to level with you. We spent most of our budget for last year on easels and graphite pencils and we haven't paid our dues for the new year yet. We don't have a ton of money for this. Plus, you want us to buy a bunch of drugs to sedate these things. I understand your concerns. Pete says these guys are about 190 lb each, so

I get it. But he's also taken care of them all week and still has all ten of his fingers, so how dangerous can they be. I think you're worrying too much. We'll scrap the steaks and the dog idea. What if you held up a mirror to them so they think you're one of them?

JON > I've asked about a dozen times. Please make an offer of an hourly rate and then we'll continue.

ME > Fair. We can give you 75 an hour starting once you administer the sedatives.

PETE SAID HE HAS SOME TRANQ DARTS, I DON'T KNOW WHY. ALL YOU HAVE TO DO IS CRAWL INTO THE CAGE AND SHOOT THEM INTO THEIR NECKS AND THEY SHOULD BE ASLEEP IN ABOUT 5-10 MINUTES.

JON > I got $75/hr for my last gig, a solo nude photo shoot, and $80/hr for the one before that which was another solo nude photo shoot. Since we're using large, illegal, exotic lizards and I'll be caged, can you make a better offer?

ME > This is a solo nude photo shoot, it's just you and the lizards, solo and nude.

JON > The lizards (and cage). That's why I'm asking you to increase your offer.

ME > Yup naked (and alone in the cage), like I said.

JON > Due to the added risk of catching a disease from them - even sedated - how's 125/hr sound?

ME > Ok, update. Pete only has one tranq dart. So one will be sedated and the other will be wide awake. Sure we can do a $125/hour rate, but we'll have to cut our time in half. Is that cool?

JON > So like $60?

Date and location?

ME > Ok so we're clear. You will come, climb into the enclosure with two wide awake 190 lb Komodo dragons. We will take away the ladder so no one can escape. You will shoot one of them with a tranquilizer dart which will take a few minutes to set in. That Komodo dragon will fall asleep. Beginning once he is asleep, you will have 30 minutes on the clock to pose with the fully conscious Komodo dragon as well as the other sleeping Komodo dragon. You will "faux" wrestle with the unconscious one, whatever that means, and playfully wrestle with the fully conscious one. We will not give you any sort of meat or dog or mirror distractions to taunt the deadly lizards with. You will figure it out and make it work for $60. We can still have a safe word. Does this all sound good?

JON > Let's make it $100 and I'm not stepping foot in there until it's asleep. Make sure they're WELL fed.

"PETE WAS FEEDING THE DRAGONS THIS
AFTERNOON AND THERE WAS A SMALL MISHAP."

ME ⟩ Hey, sorry for the delay but there's been a slight change of plans. Rescheduling. Pete was feeding the dragons this afternoon and there was a small mishap. No worries, we think he's going to be fine, but he definitely can't host this weekend. New date TBD, I'll keep you in the loop.

Need a date for company holiday party

Long story short, I told a little white lie a couple of years back at a work event about a guy I was seeing. It felt harmless at the time, but since then the little lie has sort of spiraled and now I'm in too deep. I've run out of excuses as to why this dream man can't attend my work functions and everybody thinks we're newly engaged at this point. So I'm looking for someone to play my fiancé at this year's holiday party. It's in a few weeks so you'll have some time to prep. There is a lot to know.

Fill me in. I'll provide the service. Sell the dream to your coworkers.

ME › Great. I'm freaking out at this point. Do you think you'll be able to convincingly meet 200 people as my fiancé? You need to be up for a bit of acting. And I need to know you'll be good on your toes.

PAUL › Alright, I'll try to break this down in questions to hit main points in case they ask. I don't drink so I can stay on my toes as I cater to you. Now the key is not to be too PDA with it if we've been together for a long time. I'll cater to you as a gentleman would but it's also important to know how you built this fiancé and meet those expectations. This will be fun.

Name, birthday, favorite food and drink?

Where and how did we meet?

Who at the party do we "know"?

How long have you been working at this company?

Who are your closest coworkers?

Do you have a ring?

When is the wedding date?

Anything else I should know, fill me in. Looking forward to this.

My best,
Paul

ME › Your attention to detail is impressive. I'm starting to feel a little better about my lies. Here we go...

My name is Maya, my birthday is September 14. I love cheese a lot, but I also love a good juice cleanse. I'm gonna go ahead and count juice cleansing as eating, so my favorite drink is a gin martini. Funnily enough, gin martinis are what got me into this mess.

We met at a bar in Paris.

We know mostly everyone at the firm as my father is a partner and also thinks you're real—FYI. I know this is completely insane. We should try to avoid him as much as possible but I have no doubt that he'll pull you aside at some point so be prepared for that.

I've been at the company for five years.

The coworkers I'm closest to are Alison and John. Only Alison knows you're not real and she thinks it's hilarious. She may try to throw us some curve balls for her own amusement so you should probably try to avoid her too. This is actually a legitimate concern of mine.

Yes, I bought myself a diamond ring. It's beautiful, please hold your judgement.

The wedding is next fall, we don't have a date yet because we can't decide on a New York or a Paris wedding. I think either will be beautiful.

YOU SHOULD ALSO KNOW THAT WE MOVED IN TOGETHER ABOUT A YEAR AGO. AND TWO MONTHS AGO WE TOOK A TRIP TO AFRICA, WHERE YOU PROPOSED AT THE TOP OF MOUNT KILIMANJARO. IF YOU HAVE ANY MORE QUESTIONS JUST KEEP THEM COMING.

PAUL > You definitely went for the hail mary with this one. As I read this I found it incredibly funny but insane at the same time. I get it, I've definitely dragged out a few white lies, but Mount Kilimanjaro? A bar in Paris at least makes sense. But proposing up there, I'm not even physically fit! LMAO, but let's run with it. Tell Alison not to OD lol.

ME > I know, I know. I'm really just thankful that you're amused by this to be honest...

PAUL > OK, When is the company party?

What date did we meet? and the name of the bar?

What's your father's name and the name of the company?

What are things you do constantly at home that your dad would know about?

Word for word tell me how you told the story of this proposal. I'll try to deflect everyone because it's still a party and will make it more fun than have convo but am definitely aware of what's coming.

My main concern is your dad and having that convo with him as to why I didn't ask him for your hand in marriage. lol

Luckily I have friends from Tanzania so we can run with the Mt. Kilimanjaro trip.

Do you have a picture you can send?

ME > The company party is next Thursday, so we're getting close. I think my chest will be tight until then.

We met in early November of 2013. It was the wee hours so it could have been Nov. 7 or Nov. 8. You were so caught up dancing and falling in love with me, you didn't think to check the time.

Honestly, I'd feel more comfortable telling you my father's full name and the name of the firm closer to the date, but I will tell you that his first name is Joseph and it is a legal firm based out of Manhattan.

THINGS I DO CONSTANTLY AT HOME...
I MAKE A LOT OF TEA, I LEAVE DIRTY
SOCKS AROUND THE APARTMENT
WHICH HE KIND OF ALWAYS USED TO
YELL AT ME FOR, AND I HAVE FAIRLY
FREQUENT NIGHT TERRORS YOU
SHOULD PROBABLY BE AWARE OF.

I didn't tell the proposal story in too much detail. I really just said that we got to the top of the mountain on our trek and you surprised me. Our guide was in on it and took photos on your phone, which you then lost on that same trip. Such a bummer. Feel free to add any details to the story that you want. I'll act like I love hearing you tell the story every time.

As for my dad, we can avoid him for as long as possible, but he's definitely going to want to know why it's the first time you're meeting and why you didn't ask for my hand. I haven't quite worked that out yet so give it some thought.

And finally, just google Mount Kilimanjaro and a ton of photos will come up.

PAUL > Oh damn I had no idea I was French. We're definitely scrapping that part. I'm a cinematographer that worked on a shoot and had a night off to where we met at the bar in (whatever city in France you were in) I'm usually traveling a lot on shoots so I never had the opportunity to meet him nor ask for your hand in marriage. That'll give you some leeway and no one will ask much after that.

I already looked up Mt Kilimanjaro so we're solid on that. Now for the personal stuff if you don't mind...

Were you with anyone on this Paris trip?

What do you like to dance to?

You're stuck on an island and only have 5 albums you cherish with you. What albums are they?

What's your favorite past time?

What got you into law?

What are you aspiring to become?

If you have any questions please feel free to ask. They may quiz you too lol

Please send me a picture

ME > Oh my god. I love that idea about your being a cinematographer, but I actually told them you're a cardiothoracic surgeon and you were attending med school in Paris when we met.

Now to answer your questions...

Let's be honest, there was no Paris trip. It was another lie.

There won't be much dancing at this party so I wouldn't worry about it.

Why am I stuck on an island with five albums? Does this mean my phone is working? I'm likely not listening to music, I'm trying to get a Wifi signal so that I can phone authorities.

If my colleagues ask, my favorite pastimes are cycling classes and painting.

What got me into law was pressure from my entire family especially my dad. He's a total hard ass and nothing is ever good enough for him.

I am aspiring to get through this night without anyone catching me in this lie.

I've attached a picture of Mount Kilimanjaro for your reference since you refuse to just Google it.

PAUL > You're killing me here. This gets deeper and deeper. lol

And I meant a picture of yourself. I would like to know who I'm lying for. I was asking a hypothetical question to

"I AM ASPIRING TO GET THROUGH THIS NIGHT
WITHOUT ANYONE CATCHING ME IN THIS LIE."

loosen you up about the island, and I already looked up Mt. Kilimanjaro but if you do have a moment to send a quick pic or if you have Instagram, tell me your handle.

If there's anything else I need to know about this dream guy, feel free to fill me in. I have to start doing my cardiothoracic surgeon research.

ME >
THERE ARE A FEW MORE THINGS...
YOU HAVE A GLUTEN ALLERGY SO
YOU SHOULD PROBABLY STAY AWAY
FROM MOST OF THE FOOD. YOU'RE A
JUDO BLACK BELT, YOU SPEAK FOUR
LANGUAGES, AND RYAN GOSLING IS
YOUR THIRD COUSIN. AND I THINK I
KNOW THE ANSWER BUT WOULD YOU
POSSIBLY BE WILLING TO GET A TATTOO
OF MY INITIALS ON YOUR HAND....

PAUL > This has to be a joke. I only speak 2 languages so hopefully no one speaks to me in different dialect.

Ryan Gosling? lol

I hate to ask but I have to, what compensation for all this were you thinking of?

How many people have you told this story to? Just wondering.

And definitely a no go on a tat.

ME > Probably like 100 to 150 people are expecting to meet you and know the story. Now, we have to figure out this tattoo situation.

PAUL > Marker or henna. No tat.

ME > A henna will look obvious. I will pay for the tattoo and it will be really subtle, I promise. We're getting down to the wire and I'm really starting to panic. You got measured for your tux and all, right? By the way, over the weekend we looked at houses in Westchester. We're looking to buy.

PAUL > Yea sorry, that's a no on the tattoo. It's a bit much. Everything already sounds crazy and adding permanent ink to my body that's not my choice is asking for a lot. And I wasn't aware it was a tuxedo kind of party?!

ME > I mean, it's a small tattoo. And yes, the event is black tie. Didn't I tell you that?

PAUL > Sorry I must've missed it between the romantic judo surgeon and the unavoidable engagement story. That's too last minute, are you covering the suit?

ME > My chest is getting tight over here. I will pay for both...

PAUL > I ain't doing a tat.

This keeps getting more and more ridiculous with this lie getting bigger and bigger.

THIS IS STARTING TO SOUND LIKE A COMPLETE JOKE.

ME > I know it's overboard, but it's something I told people. I guess maybe we can fake the tattoo with a thin marker before the event. I just don't want to get caught...

Listen... your email earlier hit a nerve. I was a little mad before, but I'm not anymore. But I sort of did tell a few people at the end of the day that I found some emails on your computer last night. Like, bad emails. We can probably get out of this.

ME > Ok, a lot of my coworkers aren't your biggest fans right now. It all started with the emails I mentioned yesterday. We'll just have to act like we're *trying to act* like everything is fine when really we're in a huge fight because you're an asshole and you had an affair, does that make sense?

PAUL > Too many things to keep track of to be honest. I'll keep track as much as I can, hopefully it won't turn into a full blown interrogation considering this is a law firm after all.

ME > Hey.... this is a really hard thing for me to tell you even though all of it was a lie to begin with, but...

We broke up last night. I sort of just blurted it out this morning. Then I had to come up with a whole breakup story, it was exhausting. Anyway, you're moving your things out of our apartment right now and I still haven't decided if I'm going to the holiday party or not.

Breakups are hard... even when they're not real.

PAUL > Lmao!!!!!!

Look forward to some awkward encounters.

Free mattress

Full mattress. Two years old. Tainted by the genitals of my grandfather. I will give you the mattress and boxspring for free if you please come get it tonight. I cannot have it in my home for another second. I caught my grandfather "hiding his snake in the bush" with his girlfriend this morning, as he so eloquently described it when I shamefully brought it up to him, and it has been haunting me all day. I don't know where he heard that phrase, but my life is probably ruined. Apparently they have been fornicating in this bed every night for the past week without sheets. My only other option is to burn my apartment to the ground. Please come retrieve geriatric love pad at your earliest convenience.

Oh my god. I'm so sorry you had to see that. I could use this for my guest room. Is it in good condition, other than the horrible mental images? I'm checking with a friend now to see if he can help me pick it up tonight.

ME > Thanks for your condolences. My siblings are housing him next time he's in town—he's absolutely impossible.

I just gave the mattress a quick scan, and it looks like Pop Pop and his girlfriend ate leftover spaghetti in bed while I was at work last week like I asked them not to. I'm going to try to spot treat this tomato sauce stain. Would be great if you could pick it up in the next day or two. The sooner I never have to see it again, the better.

FRAN > I'm not sure it's worth it with the tomato sauce stains. How big?

ME > Well, I managed to get the sauce out almost completely. I think if you just flip it, it'll be like new. Did your friend answer about picking it up tonight? I have a Sleepy's delivery scheduled for tomorrow morning.

FRAN > If I pick it up tonight, where will you sleep? I don't think I can come by tonight, but if it's a deal breaker I will try to find a way. How big was the stain?

ME > Don't worry about me, I've been sleeping on the pullout in my living room since I gave them my room for the week. I just wanted to get rid of the mattress ASAP, but you can pick it up whenever works for you. The sauce stain was about the size of a closed fist but now it's super light, plus it smells like Febreeze. Throw some sheets on this thing and you're golden.

FRAN > Ok great, that sounds good. Tomorrow works, what time?

ME > Ok so I was lifting the mattress to move it into the hallway and I noticed there was a red wine spill on the other side. A bottle of Chianti did mysteriously go missing a day after he got here so there's that mystery solved. He must have flipped the mattress to hide it from me, which also explains what happened to my sheets. I'm going to treat this stain and let it soak overnight and then tomorrow you can come anytime after 5 to pick it up and it should be dry by then.

FRAN > How big is this stain? Is it really noticeable? I'm not sure if this is worth it.

IT'S SHOCKING THAT THIS ALL HAPPENED IN ONE WEEK.

ME > It's pretty noticeable, in fact it looks like he spilled the entire bottle. Don't worry, I'm going to get going on this right now so this mattress will look good as new by the time you pick it up tomorrow.

FRAN > I don't think you're going to get it out, and it definitely won't be as "good as new." I'm scared that it smells at this point too. I think I need to pass on this, I would hate knowing that my guests are sleeping on these massive stains. Throw it out on the street and move on.

ME > Fran, trust me on this. This is a good mattress. It's two years old. To throw it out would be a waste of over a grand. I'm willing to give it to you for free. I spot treated the stains, I've dumped an entire bottle of Febreeze on it so if anything, the bolognese and wine smells are completely masked by Mediterranean lavender at this point. And like I said, you can just cover the sauce, wine, and footprint stains with a sheet.

FRAN › Uh... footprints? Is this a joke?

ME › No, I noticed some footprints on the perimeter of the mattress when I was trying to remove the wine stain, like he was walking around on it? Your guess is as good as mine. Anyway, like I said, just throw a sheet over it. You can come pick it up whenever you want, but tonight would be great. It's still really wet but if you tie it to the roof of your car it'll probably dry faster. It'll also probably air it out some, which would be for the best.

FRAN › Ok, I'm going to have to pass on this. You really shouldn't describe something as "good" condition when there are weird stains all over it. I definitely don't want my friends sleeping on something that needs to be "aired out."

ME › Well, I put it on the street this morning and there was already someone asleep on it when I got home today so... I don't think I need to tell you that you missed out on an incredible opportunity.

Beggin' for Beggin' Strips

I think this is a pretty simple job. I need someone who would be willing to make a weekly run to Petco for me to stock up on Purina Beggin' Strips. It would just be a bag or two a week, preferably of the bacon and cheese flavor. I'd do it myself, but I can't go to the one near my apartment anymore since the manager figured out I don't have a dog. I'd just need you to pick up the strips and deliver them to my apartment, where I'll have you feed them to me for doing tricks. Serious inquiries only please. I've been toyed with enough.

I'll pick them up for you for $100 a bag you freak

ME > Ugh. Honestly, that's steep. But you're the only one who's replied so maybe I'll do it. You better be willing to toss them into my mouth for that price.

When are you available?

WES > How about tonight

ME > Take back the freak comment...

WES > Fine

ME > Say it...

WES > I take back saying you're a freak

ME > Thanks

WES > Why do you eat dog food

ME › It's not dog food. It's a dog treat. You've never tasted a Beggin' Strip, that's pretty obvious.

WES › Yeah, I don't eat dog food.

ME › Treats*

WES › Whatever dude, so what are the details. What do I need to do.

ME › Bring me the treats, hello? And watch me devour them.

WES › I don't need to watch.

ME ›
LIKE HELL YOU DON'T. YOU DELIVER
ME THE MEATY TREATS, MAKE ME
DO TRICKS, AND WATCH AS I GOBBLE
THEM UP. THAT'S THE DEAL.

WES › What is wrong with you bro. Can we meet up somewhere so I know you're real.

ME › Ok but you need to pick a place that is nowhere near Petco, please be diligent about finding a location because I cannot be seen by the store manager. By the way are you ok with the tricks thing.

WES › Omg. What tricks.

ME › Sit, lie down, paw, sit pretty. Possibly fetch.

WES > No. And I don't want to watch you eat dog food either.

ME > Ok, you really need to stop calling it dog food.

WES > Too weird. Forget it.

ME > Apologize to me right now.

Volunteers for free cryotherapy

Hey, I am trying to start my own cryotherapy business from my apartment and in order to get it off the ground, I'm going to need some volunteers to come in and give it a shot for free. I've created a full body chamber in my shower using an ice maker and an air conditioner. Email if interested and I will explain in further detail. You won't find a deal like this on Groupon.

I am interested - what does it entail?

ME ⟩ Hey there. Thanks for reaching out. First of all, are you familiar with the many benefits of cryotherapy?

JESSE ⟩ Not really. It reduces pain right?

ME ⟩ Where do I begin? It's true... cryotherapy can be used to heal injuries or sore muscles, but that's not all. It can also slow down signs of aging and help burn hundreds of calories, potentially boosting your metabolism.

Think I'm finished? Because I'm not. Cryotherapy can also reduce anxiety and depression. Have eczema? Cryotherapy can reduce the symptoms. Worried about dementia? Guess what? Cryotherapy can prevent it.

JESSE ⟩ That seems like a lot, but I also don't have any of those issues...

ME ⟩ Ok well it can also simply enhance health and wellness overall. If you're interested, I can just tell you about my process.

JESSE > Sure, I'd be open to hearing about it.

ME > Ok, so a normal session is about 2-3 min long, not including set up. Since my chamber is homemade, the set up takes a little bit longer. I'll be conducting the session in my standup shower at home. There's a glass door that shuts securely and a space between the ceiling and shower for access. The way it will work is you'll step into a cold shower and I'll lock you inside. I've mounted a portable air conditioner and aimed it down to hit you directly from above.

JESSE > Is that it?

ME > No, once you're locked into the shower with the AC blasting down on you, I'll begin to manually dump buckets of ice cubes into the shower from above. You can opt to wear a helmet. I've invested in an industrial ice machine (like the ones you see in hotels) so I will have large quantities of ice on hand. When the shower is mostly filled with ice, I'll turn the timer on for 2-3 min.

JESSE > So what you're saying is that I will be in your shower in a helmet as you dump ice cubes on my head?

ME > I'm not aiming for your head. I'm just dumping buckets of them from over you so one or two might land on your head. And the helmet is completely optional.

JESSE > What is the purpose of this exactly?

ME > Do you remember all of the benefits I mentioned earlier?

JESSE > How many people have done this with you before?

ME > You would be the first. I tried giving myself the treatment and things went awry. You need someone to be standing outside the shower to manually dump the ice.

I TRIED TO FASHION AN OVERHEAD ICE DISPENSER AND I GOT A SCRATCHED CORNEA FROM A CUBE HITTING ME IN THE EYE. I WOULD DEFINITELY RECOMMEND WEARING GOGGLES AT LEAST. SO WHEN DO YOU WANT TO DO THIS?

JESSE > I don't know - it seems a little dangerous...

ME > Just wear the goggles and helmet if you feel that way. Honestly, the benefits of cryotherapy outweigh the dangers of my makeshift chamber. The only thing I could see maybe being worried about is if my shower door gets jammed again and you're trapped under 200 lbs of ice for a little while, but I really don't think that's going to happen.

JESSE > Wait....'jammed again'? This is sounding more and more dangerous. Not really seeing the benefits of this for me.

ME › Don't worry about that. Look, if the door gets stuck, I will pass you a hairdryer over the top of the glass to melt the ice.

JESSE › Now you're passing me a blow dryer in a shower? This is absurd. No thanks.

ME › ONLY if the door jams.

JESSE › This is ridiculous. No thanks...

Personal "chef"

Basically, I'm looking for someone to come over at night to nuke and plate my TV dinners to make eating them less depressing. Just come over, pop the meal in the micro and arrange it on a plate in a way that is pleasing. Maybe add a sprig of parsley. I dunno. Make it look like it would in a restaurant. I know I could do this myself, but there's just something incredibly pathetic about that. Don't feel bad, I love frozen dinners. They're just depressing. I'll also pay you to stay while I eat it... My god, I am so fucking pathetic.

I can actually cook! So if you would like to discuss weekly food options that can be prepared in your home or mine and delivered please let me know. You pay for cost of food, reusable containers and I am paid an hourly fee for my time.

Thank you.

ME > Awesome. I have enough options for several weeks and they all come in plastic trays that I am pretty sure are 100% recyclable. You can come for however many hours you want. How are your plating skills on a scale from 1 to 10?

CATHY > 5-7 plating depending on food. You did see I have an hourly rate for this.

ME > Yes, I did. Cathy, I have to say I'm a bit distracted by that 5-7. Plating and presentation skills are probably the most important part of this job since most of this food has the exact consistency of gruel.

IF I DON'T BELIEVE I AM EATING IN A FIVE-STAR RESTAURANT I'M NOT SURE IT'S WORTH IT FOR ME TO PAY SOMEONE TO PLATE IT FOR ME. MAYBE THERE IS A WAY TO BRING THIS AVERAGE RATING OF YOURS UP TO A 9 OR A 10. DO YOU DABBLE WITH GARNISHES?

CATHY > Thanks for getting back to me. Sounds like you really need a food stylist. I am a cook/chef. I don't normally serve. I execute recipes etc. Good luck.

ME > But you will also be cooking the meals?

CATHY > Yes, you and I can discuss what you might like as I have no way of knowing. I can cook at your house or mine. I have NOT worked in restaurants. I can provide references. I can keep kitchen organized and make sure you have groceries and what is needed in pantry. I have another business as well that doesn't involve food. I handle people's personal/biz life.

Thanks.

ME > Ok great. So I really love the Thanksgiving style meals with turkey and stuffing and this cranberry paste-like gook... it comes with this brown stuff I assume is gravy. My second favorite would probably be fish sticks and mashed potatoes with mixed up peas, carrots, and corn. There's this meatloaf one that I also really like that comes with peas and mashed potatoes. Mashed potatoes are pretty much a staple in these things. I have a bunch of all of these in the freezer now so you won't have to worry about restocking for a while.

CATHY > So to clarify: You are ok for now but you would potentially want me to cook what you listed or similar in the future?

ME > No, that is what I want you to cook for me now. But you don't have to buy any of the ingredients because I have them all. They are all in the tray you will be cooking in the microwave. Unless you want to add some garnishes. Does that make sense?

CATHY > Is this food already cooked or you just need plating? Sorry not clear

ME > It needs to be heated in the microwave and then plated beautifully. Add maybe a garnish or two. And then there's the matter of serving it to me restaurant style.

CATHY > And what are you paying for this service??

ME > Well it depends on whether you do this long term or not. How authentic are you willing to make my experience? How will you garnish the plate? At this point

I should mention I have a severe allergy to parsley. Do you know how to use an epipen?

CATHY > I'm sorry I just don't think we are on the same page here.

Good luck.

SIX MONTHS LATER I POSTED THE SAME AD...

CATHY > I'm going to try again. We've chatted prior. Why not just hire a personal chef? Better quality of food AND exactly what you want. Left overs won't be a drag. Food shopping as well.

ME > Cathy, Cathy, Cathy... You know I love the taste of my TV dinners. Plus I have like a million of them in my freezer now. I would really hate for those to go to waste. How are your plating skills these days? If I remember correctly, they were a bit low on the plating scale. I take it you've been brushing up?

CATHY > Finish the frozen "nasty" and then you should at least try me for 1 shop & cook.

ME > What is the nasty?

CATHY > The "nasty" = processed TV dinners. As opposed to all fresh and homemade.

ME > Forgive me, my slang is not up to date. Yeah these dinners are nasty and fresh for sure. I don't think you answered the whole garnish question. Would you be able to dress up a plate with a garnish? Some herbs or a light drizzle on the dish? Most of the meals come with pretty liquid-y sauces.

CATHY > I could but honestly not enough $$. If you decide you'd like to try some real food let me know.

ME > Is it the whole microwave thing? Honestly they're very easy to operate. You just push the numbers to set the time you want to cook the dinner for.

CATHY > Gross.

House sitter needed for upstate manor

Escape the city for a few days and relax in the middle of nature. It's like renting an Airbnb, but it's free. All you have to do is look after a few things… very easy. You will have the run of the estate, pool, and liquor cabinet. Just follow the rules (which I will share), respect the furniture, and please water my plants. The house is situated in a heavily wooded area with a ton of privacy and nature right at your fingertips.

Hi, my name is Lisa. I'd be ecstatic to sit your home. It sounds like a great opportunity to get some peace and quiet and meditation, which I could use. I actually really love plants. I helped plant flowers in the community garden last weekend so your babies will be fine with me. I hope to hear from you soon. If you'd like you can give me a call.

ME > Hello. Nice to hear from you Lisa. I have to head out of town next week so I would need you to go up to my house and... keep an eye on things. Ideally you could arrive Monday and stay the week. If you are able to do that, I will tell you a bit more about the house and the grounds.

LISA > Yes, I would be able to do that. Please tell me more. I'm excited. lol

ME > Ok. Will it just be you?

LISA > Yes

ME > Ok. I will send you a code for the security gate and I will leave a key beside the third gargoyle on the veranda. This key is to the front door. There is a second key that is for the shed in the backyard. You shouldn't need to get into the shed but I'll leave the key on the key ring just in case. So the house is quite large... thirteen bedrooms, most of them are empty and unused. You can take your pick of any of them except one. You will know which one it is because it is locked with a red X painted on the door. There are plants in the study and the kitchen that need watering.

LISA > Okay, do you have any pets that need tending?

ME > No pets. And by the way, if you see a cloaked figure roaming around the property at any point, it is likely the groundskeeper, Allen. He has a horrible allergy to the sun and keeps his face and skin covered entirely at all times.

LISA > Okay, what's the address and if I get a little lonely can I bring my friend?

ME > Yes, but just the one friend. And you should tell them everything I am telling you about the house. I will send you the address as soon as we are confirmed. There are a few more things you should know. This is not a big deal but there is sometimes a draft in the study. I don't

know why but at night it tends to get very cold in certain spots. Also, the house is very old and the pipes make quite a bit of noise so if you hear strange sounds like whispers or rapping coming from inside the walls, that's all that is.

LISA › Strange noises and men in cloaks are nothing to be afraid of nor are the whispers as long as they don't say my name. And I love to be cold so when would you like to meet?

ME › That's right, there's nothing to be afraid of at all. I just wanted to give you fair warning so there are no surprises. Also please ignore the old doll collection in the attic. They belonged to my great-aunt.

Anyway, I will not be able to meet you but like I said, I will leave the house key along with the key to the panic room right next to the third gargoyle in front of the house and you can let yourselves in.

LISA > Okay. What are the directions to the house and what's the code to the panic room? Oddly I love old dolls so no worries, I won't go snooping. I'm only there to water the plants.

ME > Oh dear, I meant to say shed.

WELL NOW YOU KNOW, THERE IS A PANIC ROOM IN THE SHED. YOU WILL HAVE THE KEY TO THIS, BUT YOU SHOULD ONLY NEED TO GO INSIDE THIS ROOM IF THERE IS AN INTRUDER OR IF ALLEN GOES OFF HIS MEDS.

The code is to open the front gate that will let you onto the property. I will give this to you next week. One more thing, do NOT, under any circumstances, go down to the basement. I cannot stress this enough. If you hear something odd, remember what I said about the pipes. If the power goes out again, the circuit breaker is located in the front foyer. Do not dare set foot in the basement no matter what.

LISA > Okay cool. Do you need me to remind Allen about his medication?

ME > I appreciate that, but it's not a good idea. Allen hears enough voices as it is. He came to me from a mental institution and does not like being confronted. Better off just leaving him be. I'm not sure if I mentioned this but there is no cell service at the house, so you and your friend will be off the grid for the week. Should be very relaxing.

Piñata wanted

We're throwing my kid a birthday party this weekend.
Looking for someone to come be a human piñata.
Totally get it's weird, but it's what he wants and well,
we like to spoil him a little bit on his birthday.

Good Evening,

I hope this message finds you well. My name is Dan and I would like to help make your son's birthday extra special by being a human piñata. Yes, I realize it's a bit of a different gig, but I take all work seriously and I've worked in an elementary school for the past 6 years so I'm used to how quirky kids can be. lol

I have attached my resume which includes my picture. If you are interested, you can reach me here or at xxx-xxxx. Thank you and have a great weekend!

ME > Hey Dan, thanks for your email. Sounds like you might be just the guy for the job. Do you own any sort of costumes by any chance? Or multicolored clothing you could wear? The visual I have in my head is that rainbow donkey look, but really I guess a piñata could be anything.

DAN > Hmmm... I don't have anything specifically multi colored, but if you give me 10 minutes I can put some outfits on and send pics? I am going to try to combine my most colorful garments!

A FEW MINUTES LATER...

DAN > Okay so I managed to make 2 outfits. As you will see, one of them is an ugly Christmas suit. I know it's not Christmas, but it's very colorful. Let me know what you think.

ME > Ok sure, that works. We can wrap you in party streamers if you look nothing like a piñata. How much do you weigh if you don't mind my asking? Trying to figure out the rig.

DAN > Sounds good! I am 159 lbs.

ME >
OK SO HANGING YOU FROM OUR CEILING FAN IS PROBABLY NOT A GREAT IDEA.

It might hold you but I don't want to take any chances. There's some scaffolding out in front of our building I might be able to suspend you from if there's no construction going on that day. Basically you just have to hang there and let them hit you. If they get in a good whack, toss some candy and watch 'em go nuts.

DAN > I understand, and I certainly would not want to ruin your ceiling fan. And here I thought I was lean! Lol. And okay sounds good. I can throw candy for every hit and I'll even throw in some silly puns here and there as well. When were you looking to have the party?

ME > This Saturday. And good news... I touched base with the construction company and they don't work on Saturdays so the scaffolding is all ours. We'll figure out how to get you up there. Best way might be to tie one end of a rope around your waist and the other to the back of my pickup truck and pull up the street.

DAN > That might be the best way. Perhaps some clips to my waist as well the way rock climbers do it, or by manipulating the rope around my waist and under my arms.

Everything sounds great. Here's hoping it doesn't rain that day!

ME > Same here buddy. So listen, the party starts at noon, we'll be doing the piñata after lunch which puts us at about 2 PM. I have to figure out how the hell to get you up there using the clips so let's start early so I can spend the rest of the morning worrying about the rest of the party. Can you get here around 7? I'll have you hanging up there by 8/8:30. I have a feeling once the guests arrive it's going to be mayhem.

DAN > Okay, so this coming Saturday, arrival at 7. Sounds good. I'm going to mark this into my schedule now. I am also going to speak to some friends and see if they have ideas in regards to how to be hung up there, utilizing a scaffold.

ME > Yeah, maybe bring a book to read while you're hanging up there since you'll have a few hours to kill.

DAN > Hey! Sorry, hectic weekend. But sounds good. I'll either bring a book or use my phone!

ME > Ok great. And listen, I have to warn you, a couple of our neighbors are a little bat shit. The woman right below us is the worst. She hates kids so she'll do anything to spoil their fun.

ANYWAY, YOU'LL PROBABLY BE DANGLING RIGHT OUTSIDE HER WINDOW FOR A WHILE IN THE MORNING SO IF SHE COMES OVER AND BOTHERS YOU, DO ME A FAVOR AND JUST PRETEND YOU'RE A WINDOW WASHER AND TELL HER TO MIND HER BUSINESS. I'LL GIVE YOU A SQUEEGEE TO KEEP ON YOU SO IT'S MORE BELIEVABLE.

DAN > LOL okay. I mean I do tend to be a bit of a charmer, so perhaps I can sweet talk her while up there. Some old ladies just wanna feel young again :)

ME > She's a real piece of work, this one. She once complained to our landlord that my son was riding his scooter around the apartment making a racket. He doesn't even have a scooter. He's sixteen. My main concern is that she'll call the cops—we'll need to have a plan for if she does.

DAN > Well hopefully her and the rain stay away!

ME > Yeah, Dan, we're gonna have this party rain or shine so hope you're on board to get slightly soaked. As for Mrs. Henderson, my main concern is the police showing up again if she complains. Really something I don't need to deal with on Saturday so if you wouldn't mind just taking one for the team and dealing with the cops, that would be awesome.

DAN > Quite an amount of stuff going on. How much does the gig pay?

ME > I can't say that I've ever hired anyone to do something like this before. Not sure how to price it. What do you think?

DAN > Well it is odd to price, and there are a number of factors that play into it (7-3 time slot, hung from a scaffold in public during a rainy day and exposed to not only your neighbor but potential malicious passersby, possibly dealing with law enforcement and finally dealing with a 16 year old beating me with no safe word as opposed to a younger child).

So with all of those factors involved, I was thinking $250.

ME > Dan, I'll level with you. Yes, it is supposed to downpour on Saturday and yes my neighbor is a nightmare, but to be honest, you're really only working for about 20 minutes. The rest of the time is free for you to do with as you please... read a book, do a crossword, take a nap. And not sure I'll be able to lower you until around 8 pm by the way but like I said, hang out and do whatever you want.

DAN > Wait, so even though the piñata aspect is 20 min, I would be literally hanging up there from 8 AM - 8 PM?

ME > Correct. There's a lot going on that day man. I'll be chasing after about thirty teenagers. I can't be fussing with a crane until everyone has been picked up by a parent and I'm no longer responsible for them.

Tea Party

Growing up, I had a ton of dolls. I used to ritually brush their hair and have tea parties with them every single day. Now that I'm an adult, and my childhood dolls have been taken from me, I'm looking for someone who will come over and let me brush their hair and have tea parties with me. We can even put real vodka in the cups instead of just pretending. When I finish all the vodka, I'm DEFINITELY going to want to brush your hair. Email me if you're interested in helping me recreate the days of my childhood.

Hello,

My name is Ashley. I'm replying to your Craigslist ad. I found it interesting. In my childhood I would dress up my plushies, take them out for walks and make homes for them. I would gladly help you recreate your tea parties from childhood. I can make real tea and I'm good at baking.

Cheers

ME > Hi Ashley, thanks for your email. I would love for you to join my tea party. Let me tell you a little bit about them. What I usually do is set up a small table in my apartment with some dolls that I keep in a box under my bed and you in a cute dress that I will lend you. I'll set up a small spread with some finger foods and cups filled with vodka. You can have tea if you'd like, but I like to sip straight vodka. Then we'll have quiet time for about an hour while I brush your hair 100 strokes. Let me know if you have any other questions, happy to answer.

ASHLEY > Sounds great. When were you planning this for?

ME > I'll have to check my roommates' schedules. They seriously hate when I do this so I usually like to schedule it for when I know they won't be home. Do you like vodka?

ASHLEY > Oh okay. Keep me posted.

I do like vodka, but only if mixed with something. But again I would like to brew some tea. Since it is a tea party.

ME > You and this tea. Ok, sure. I'll 100% be drinking vodka.

I WAS WONDERING, WOULD YOU
BE WILLING TO WEAR LONG FAKE
EYELASHES LIKE MY DOLLS HAD? THEY
HAD THESE EYELIDS THAT OPENED
AND SHUT WHEN YOU MOVED THEM
AND THESE LONG BEAUTIFUL LASHES.
I MISS THEM SO MUCH AND IT
WOULD MEAN THE WORLD.

ASHLEY > Hey! You can put a little bit of vodka in my tea. Yes, I'll wear eyelashes. Will you provide them?

ME > Yes, I will glue them onto your eyelids when we are getting you ready. I used to sometimes draw fake eyeballs on my doll's eyelids so they could stay awake forever. Can I do that to you too? We'll probably need about half an hour to get you ready.

ASHLEY > Yes, that's fine.

ME > Ok great! So I will glue lashes on and then draw eyeballs onto your lids with black permanent marker. Would you mind if I put a little bit of blush and light pink lipstick on you too? That would really complete the look.

ASHLEY > Yes, that's okay! Anything else I should know?

ME > Ok great! Yes, there's more. My mother used to get furious at me for doing this to my dolls so I can't even believe I'm asking, but sometimes I used to take markers and scribble lines all over their arms, legs, and faces. I don't know why I did this, all I know is that it was really fun. Would I be able to draw all over you with markers after I brush your hair for a while? Something tells me it would feel really satisfying, especially after the amount of vodka I'll have had.

ASHLEY > Sure but for my body can it be washable markers rather than permanent?

ME > It has to be permanent marker or it's not the same.

ASHLEY > Sigh, okay.

ME > Well, not if you're going to huff and puff about it.

LOOK, YOU'LL BE SO COMPLETELY WASTED ON SPIKED TEA, YOU WON'T EVEN CARE THAT I AM SCRIBBLING CRAZY LINES ALL OVER YOUR BODY IN BLACK PERMANENT MARKER. TRUST ME!

ASHLEY > I guess you're right.

ME > I am right. Just wondering if you've had a haircut or a trim recently?

ASHLEY > No. Why?

ME > Sometimes I used to give my dolls haircuts......

ASHLEY > Haircuts is where I draw the line, I like my hair how it is now.

ME > Ok. What about a trim... I really would like to cut it so badly.

ASHLEY > I could wear a wig and you may cut that, BUT my real hair, out of the question.

ME > Oh honey, I am not cutting my beautiful wigs.

Help finding cell phone

We're going to need to act quickly. Long story short, I was going through my boyfriend's phone to delete an unflattering nudie of myself this morning when he was getting ready for work. I knew he'd be pissed so when he walked into the kitchen looking for his phone, I panicked and shoved it into a lasagna. Since he was running late, he decided to leave for work without it. I'm catering a large party tonight, so I made 50 lasagnas, cooked half of them, and have no idea which one the cell phone is in. I need someone to come over and help me gently sift through all 50 lasagnas to find this phone before he gets home from work.

Haha! I'm sorry but this is too funny. If you're serious, I can come over and help you find the phone.

ME > 1 sec sauce on hands

CASEY > Lol ok

ME > Hi. Sorry about that. I've been digging through lasagnas all morning. Now I'm using Siri so I don't have to touch my phone. Hopefully she cooperates for once and my messages send like normal. I could really use your help. There is literally sauce everywhere. Has anything like this ever happened to you? Send. Yes. Send. Send. Siri send.

CASEY > I can't say that I have. I've lost my phone before but never anything like this. How did this happen???

ME > I didn't hear my boyfriend get out of the shower this morning. When he walked into the kitchen he startled me and so I just shoved the phone in the first place I could find. Then I had to act natural while he had his breakfast so I just kept making lasagnas and lost track of the phone.

CASEY > Oh my god, that is too funny. Was the photo that bad? Why did you send it to him in the first place?

ME > I did not send him this picture. He took it of me while I was sleeping. My mouth is wide open and I am drooling. It is the worst picture ever taken.

CASEY > And I thought me and my boyfriend were crazy! I hear you though. That photo has to go. I would be pissed! Do you need my help?

ME > Yes. Do you think you'd be able to very gently peel through the layers of lasagna to look for the phone? You have to be very careful. I've already ruined two trays and I really don't have time to make new ones.

SIRI WHAT IS THE FASTEST WAY TO DISSECT A COOKED LASAGNA? SIRI HOW DO I DECONSTRUCT A LASAGNA?

CASEY > Lol I think I would be, but have you tried calling the phone?

ME > Not even worth it. He of course keeps his phone on silent, making my life difficult without even trying. Send. Send. Send. Fucking send.

CASEY > Why don't you try poking something thin into the lasagnas like a toothpick or a chopstick to see if you hit the phone? If you need me to come, I can.

ME > My boyfriend just called me from his office. He's coming home at lunch to look for the phone himself. He'll have a lot of questions if you're here when he gets here so we have to wait until he leaves again. Any other ideas in the mean time? Fuck me! Fuck! Delete. Siri delete email.

CASEY > Sorry, I'm all out of ideas! What happened?

ME › I dropped a tray of lasagna. My kitchen is officially a disaster area. In case you were wondering, the phone was not in the lasagna that fell...

CASEY › Hey, did you find it?

ME › No. My boyfriend is here now to look for it. He just went into the bedroom. I'm freaking out. Send. Send.

ME › Oh my god. The phone isn't on silent. It's ringing.

CASEY › I told you to call it! Did he hear it?

ME › No. I'm going to try to distract him now.

ME › Come on, where are you going? Give me a kiss. Babe I have to get back to work. I've been gone for an hour. I heard my phone ringing in here. Did you hear it? What phone? What are you talking about? My phone. It's in here. I heard it. Come on. Stop unbuttoning my shirt. I'm just happy to see you. Why are you being weird? What happened in here?

CASEY › LOL!!! You're crazy!

ME › I'm turning off Siri because she's out of control. He found the phone. It was in the oven and it's broken. He went back to work.

CASEY › Is he mad?

ME › Yes. And the picture is already in his iCloud.

CASEY › He'll get over it. It's too hysterical to stay mad. I don't know if this was real or not but it made my day. You all are nuts.

X X X

Need exterminator/ exorcist

I need someone to please come exorcise my apartment. When I first moved in six months ago, I started hearing these strange scratching sounds at night. About a month into my lease, I realized there was a rat living in the walls. He would scamper around like a mental case and keep me up for hours each night. I set some traps and after a few weeks I caught him, but I believe his spirit remained. I think he has some sort of unfinished business. I'm assuming it's a box of Triscuits I recently discovered he'd gone to town on. I still hear scratching some nights and yesterday I found some little phantom poops in one of my cabinets. If anyone has any experience in dealing with rat ghosts, I could really use your help. Will pay full expulsion price.

$100. What's your address, I can stop by tomorrow night.

ME > Hey man, thanks so much for reaching out. I've had a couple of others email about this and they really did not understand the problem or have any idea what they were talking about. This thing has kept me awake for several nights with its scampering and clawing and shrieking directly into my ear all night. How do you plan to get rid of it?

MIKE > I can stop by tomorrow evening to take a look and come up with a quick plan. I'll bring needed supplies.

ME > What are the supplies?

MIKE > Traps and stuff. Is tonight good for you?

ME > Sorry, but won't this guy just glide right through a trap?

MIKE > No—I'll definitely take care of this. Let me come—take a look set something up. If it works, you'll pay me—if not—no charge. We'll give it a couple of days to work. Let me know before 6 PM so I can set my schedule.

ME > I booked a hotel for the night since I haven't slept in so many days. I figured I needed a break from the demon, so not tonight but I'd love your help later in the week.

Here is my concern.

THIS IS NOT YOUR TYPICAL RAT
THAT CAN BE BAITED WITH CHEESE
AND CAUGHT IN A TRAP. A TRAP
WILL SNAP SHUT AND PASS RIGHT
THROUGH HIS GHOST NECK AND
HE WILL RUN FREE, POSSIBLY EVEN
ANGRIER THAN HE WAS BEFORE.
AND TRUST ME, HE'S ALREADY
VERY UPSET.

MIKE > Ok—let me know.

ME > Ok. Assuming you'll probably want to perform some sort of séance or something. If that is the case, is there anything I should get? I have sage and a Ouija board. While I don't have a photo of this particular rat, I managed to find and print one of a similar looking rat off the internet. I read that a photo of the deceased helps with this sort of thing, but you tell me.

MIKE > No—nothing like that—once I come and take a look I will be able to give an assessment.

ME > Ok. Will you perform the ritual in the same night as the "assessment"?

MIKE > Just let me know when you're available.

ME > I can be available tomorrow night but I want to make sure I'm prepared. What do I need to get? Candles? A crucifix???

MIKE > Wait—I work in Manhattan—Battery Park to East 81st. I travel the city—give me a window as to when I can pass by—let me take a look first to see exactly what's going on. Then I can let you know right then and there. You do not need candles or anything else.

ME > Hey, you are the exorcist. You know best. I just want to be completely prepared for whatever ritual it is you're coming to perform. Should I wear anything specific or no? Sorry for all the dumb questions, this is my first exorcism.

MIKE > No you don't need anything or anything special to wear.

ME > Ok, so I'm just wondering, will I be speaking directly to the rat at any point? All I know about this stuff is from researching it online but I read somewhere that it's possible that I could be talking to the poltergeist through you. Does this mean you're going to come to life as the rat, man? Because that's some scary shit. How big are you?

MIKE > No—nothing scary—let me check this out for myself first.

ME >

ARE YOU A PRIEST? I DON'T HAVE A BIBLE. WILL YOU BRING ONE?

MIKE > Stop worrying—I'll take care of it.

ME > Hey, sorry Father. I just want to be prepared. I bought like five pounds of salt. I read if you sprinkle it around it wards off evil spirits and I'm really starting to think this rat is an evil spirit, he has not let me sleep in a week. Last night at the hotel, I finally had some peace and quiet and all I could think about was the rat and the sounds it was probably making back at my apartment.

MIKE > What's your address?

ME > I booked another night in the hotel. What do you think about the salt? Is that an old wives' tale or do you think it works?

MIKE > No salt. No gimmicks or wives' tales. Just give me a time window, a date and your address.

ME > You're not gonna believe this but I got home today and I have a new live rat in my apartment. How the hell are they getting in? He ate through a box of cereal and pooped all over the counter. He ran away and now I can't find him. And it's only a matter of time before the ghost makes his presence known. Do you think they can communicate???

MIKE > Hey just let me know when I can stop by. I can't help you if I can't come by!

ME > Ok. I'm going to set traps tonight to catch this second son of a bitch because he is wreaking havoc in my pantry. I will let you know what happens, but in the event that I catch him and his soul returns like the last one, what do I do? I will be outnumbered. Is this a bad idea? You are the poltergeist/exorcism expert. Will we be able to expel two of them, YES OR NO.

MIKE ＞ Yes.

ME ＞ Mike listen, I caught the rat in a trap and drove its body out to Long Island to dispose of it far enough from my apartment that its spirit could not return. I ended up leaving it in a Sleepy's parking lot in Ronkonkoma. I'm a little worried, do you think this is going to work? Please advise.

MIKE ＞ If you hear anything, let me know. I'll come by.

Someone to keep my family in line at my 4th of July BBQ

Long story short, my family is a bunch of animals. I opened my pool this weekend and had a bunch of them over for the day on Saturday. Huge mistake. I already committed to having a 4th of July party prior to witnessing the events that transpired this past weekend. I need someone essentially to come over and keep them in line on 7/4 because I cannot do it alone. Email me and let's talk about how we do this.

Hello, very interesting ad. I'd like to know more if possible. Feel free to email or text me, xxx-xxx-xxxx.

All the Best,
Dave

ME › Hey Dave, thanks for your email. I'm at my wit's end with these barbarians. They made a goddamn mess at my place on Saturday. I've come up with some general rules for all guests as well as very explicit rules for certain family members who have a history of more specific party fouls. I can take you through each of them if you'd like. You might find this funny, and that's fine as long as you help me bring some order to my next gathering.

DAVE › I do find it a little funny, but hey I understand you have standards for people and how they act. If you'd like we can text or get on a call to discuss this.

ME > Email works best for me at the moment considering my phone ended up at the bottom of a beer cooler on Saturday, but I should have a working phone in the next few days. I'd also like you to have this stuff in writing for your reference, but closer to July 4 if you have any questions I'd be more than happy to jump on a call.

DAVE > Yeah that's all fine, if you wanna outline everything for me now that would be great.

ME > Ok, let's start with the pool and what belongs in it. Or more specifically, what does not. Loose bandaids do not. Food does not. Excrement of any kind most certainly fucking does not. I had to drain my pool on Sunday and I don't want to do it again. I need you on bandaid patrol. I picked five loose bandaids out of my pool this weekend. FIVE. No one is to go near that pool with a bandaid on. Tell me you understand this. Also, bathroom breaks are mandatory. Every half hour, especially my grandpa. Same rules apply to the hot tub.

DAVE > That all sounds reasonable. Another question is, is there compensation on my part?

ME > Yes, you tell me what you think is a good ballpark for this after you hear everything I need you to do.

DAVE > Well I'm not actually too sure. I have full confidence I can handle the crowd but I'm also factoring in that I'm kinda giving up my holiday.

ME > It's a Wednesday man, but I get it. By the way you're totally welcome to use the pool and enjoy the BBQ so long as you pay attention to everything and aren't wearing any bandaids. Let's keep going and you tell me what you think.

DAVE > Ok sounds good.

ME >

LET'S MOVE ON TO MY PARENTS. THEY'RE DIVORCED, THEY HATE EACH OTHER, AND THEY'RE BOTH COMING. YOU NEED TO KEEP THEM ON OPPOSITE SIDES OF THE YARD. I REALLY CAN'T DEAL WITH THEM GOING AT EACH OTHER LIKE THEY DID LAST WEEKEND.

Really killed the mood. Also, please make sure my mom has a full glass of Pinot Grigio at all times. She's much more pleasant when she's on the wine.

DAVE > Ok.

ME > Cool. So then there's my Uncle Ted. He's a raging alcoholic. I'm just gonna say it. If he swings at you at any point, just punch him in the face. I don't even care. If you don't feel comfortable slapping around a drunk man, lock him in a closet and I'll deal with him in the morning.

DAVE > I have no problem hitting someone lol

ME > Dude you're the man. Next: if my Aunt Edna so much as mentions politics, push her in the pool. I'm not kidding. You'll recognize her because she's the super old racist lady in a wheelchair. One word, and she's in the deep end. No excuses.

DAVE > Lol seems like this is a huge joke.

ME > Dude I'm not joking. She never makes it through a gathering without offending someone and I'm sick of it.

DAVE > Understandable.

ME > Of course it is. So we're all clear on what you need to do?

DAVE > All clear, no questions.

ME > Great. So you'll beat the shit out of my uncle and toss my 90-year-old aunt into the pool if she acts out. You'll keep my parents occupied on either end of the yard and be on high alert for any loose juicy bandaids. You know, I'm actually starting to feel a little better about this barbecue.

DAVE > I think I can handle it.

ME > Hey Dave, 911. Spoke to my dad this morning and he asked if he could bring his new girlfriend to the BBQ. I was reluctant but think she'll keep him pretty occupied. My mom on the other hand needs to be distracted. Any chance you're single?

"SO YOU'LL BEAT THE SHIT OUT OF MY UNCLE AND TOSS MY 90-YEAR-OLD AUNT INTO THE POOL IF SHE ACTS OUT."

DAVE > I'm actually not single.

ME > Well if you won't tell, I won't. I might need you to hook up with my mom, man.

ME > Ok Dave, I didn't mean to make you uncomfortable. You can say if you don't want to. I just wanted some way to keep her busy so she and my dad and Renee don't have to interact. It's a fuckin headache.

DAVE > No it's ok. I'm working so I can't always answer right away, I'll see what I can do.

ME > Ok good. My mom's a nice lady. To be honest, I was a little offended when I thought you wouldn't even be willing to give her a little kiss.

DAVE > I just have no idea who she is yet.

ME > I'll introduce you when you arrive and once the Pinot Grigio starts flowing she'll be hard to forget. Please keep her away from my dad. That's all I'm asking.

DAVE > Sounds good, have you thought about compensation?

ME > Not really, have you?

DAVE > I have but I don't want to throw out a number and offend you. I'm trying to figure out what would be fair.

ME > Dave, not to go off topic, but I've just been thinking about this and if you started dating my mom that would mean you'd be at most of our family functions and I wouldn't have to worry about this shit anymore. Are you in any way into this?

DAVE > Sounds a little extreme.

ME > I know I haven't painted my family in the best light these past few days but what family doesn't have its drama? They're a fun group dude. They're just a lot but at least we'd have each other.

DAVE > Trust me I have a huge family as well and I don't like most of them.

ME > Well it looks like you might be joining ours. Get this... I emailed my mom before to tell her about you and this is what she just replied:

> *"Wow, Dave sounds so amazing honey. I can't wait to meet him. Thank you so much for setting this up. This is going to be a holiday to remember. Hopefully your father doesn't bring that hoochie from Gwendolyn's Baptism but now even if he does it won't matter. I'll have Dave on one arm and my Pinot in the other. By the way you need to let me know what I have to bring. Did you like that potato salad I made last weekend because it looked like nobody touched it and I really don't need to waste my time."*

Dude, she's so into you.

ME >

DUDE... MY MOM WILL NOT STOP
HITTING ME UP ABOUT YOU. DO YOU
LIKE POTATO SALAD? SHE MUST HAVE
ASKED ME TEN TIMES.

DAVE > I love potato salad. How do you not have a phone yet, must drive you crazy to not be mobile.

ME > I usually like it too, but she uses way too much mayo. You should tell her. She'll listen to you... So I've been trying to figure out how to navigate this whole money situation now that we're pretty much family without it being awkward. You probably don't want to work the party anymore anyway right? Like working for your girlfriend's son... that might be weird?

DAVE > Have a good one dude. I can't entertain this anymore lol

Need urine samples

I am collecting urine samples to bring with me on an upcoming camping trip. Doesn't have to be clean. Just has to be from a human. No dog urine please. The scent of a large predator is frightening to many animals and scares them off quickly and no predator is more dangerous than a human. Sad but true. Email if interested and we can set up the exchange.

Hey if this is what it's actually being used for, then sure. Is it paid?

ME > Hi there, I assure you this is for sprinkling around the tent at my campsite. No predator will dare bother me once the scent of urine enters their nostrils. If you don't mind my asking, how many glasses of water a day would you say you drink?

ALEX > Ok. About 8 usually.

ME > Eight glasses a day! Very healthy intake. So if you are also drinking other liquids, we are talking about 2L a day. You don't do any hard drugs, do you?

ALEX > No.

ME > Good. Let's discuss a schedule. I'm thinking a couple of liters a day will put you at about 40-45 liters by the time I'm ready to take my trip. That should definitely last me for the week around camp and on my daily treks through the forest.

ALEX > That is a lot... Where are you going?

ME > It will be just enough, yes. I'm going camping in the middle of the woods so I'd like to douse the land around my tent every night to repel hungry animals. I'll also be hiking during the day and would like to fill some spray bottles to keep in my daily pack, so the more the better.

ALEX > Ok, well where are you located and how do you want to do this?

ME > You don't have to worry about that one bit. I will come to you to pick up the repellent.

ALEX > Ok, when is this trip anyway

ME > In one month.

ALEX > And how do you want to get the stuff from me?

ME > I'll come to your apartment to pick all of it up. Would you mind storing it in mason jars or glass containers? Just no plastic. It's terrible for the environment.

ALEX > Are you providing containers? When am I supposed to start doing this...

ME > Tonight would be great. I really want to make sure I have enough of the stuff to last. I'd like to very generously sprinkle it everywhere around camp if possible. I don't want any grizzly bears, wolves, or the like trying to get into my tent to eat me.

ALEX > And you'll come by when, to pick it up when?

ME > The night before my trip I will swing by to load up the car with all the jars you have saved and pay you for your services.

ALEX >

EXCUSE ME??? YOU EXPECT ME TO KEEP BOTTLES OF URINE IN MY APARTMENT FOR THE NEXT MONTH??

ME > Yes, but they will be sealed in jars. In fact, I'm starting to think canning jars would be the best idea to preserve it. Just keep them in a corner until I come.

ALEX > And tell people what????

ME > Why do you have to tell people anything? Who are these people?

ALEX > Anyone who comes to my apartment?? My roommates? What am I supposed to tell them when they ask me why there are 50 jars of pee sitting in a corner?? You must be out of your damn mind. I'm out.

ME > Just drape a sheet over the jars.

ME > Ok fine. I have to take a drug test...

Looking to barter my stuff

Just moved to the city and I'm pretty low on cash. Looking to start bartering my things. Email if you have some stuff you want to trade and we can open up the conversation. Currently, I'm looking for some kitchen items. Pots, pans, etc., but am open to other appliances as well. Let me know if you have any of these things to spare. Maybe we can turn this into a regular thing.

What kind of stuff do you have? I have some pots/pans you may be interested in...

ME > Hi Sam, thanks so much for your email. I have a bunch of things I'm willing to trade. Admittedly I have a quite sizable collection of Ty beanie babies I'm looking to unload. I think some of them could be worth something. My kitchen is totally bare. Pots and pans sound great, but do you have any kitchen appliances like a blender, mixer, anything like that?

SAM > I might have a blender, but do you have other things besides beanie babies to trade for it? I don't really have a need for them...

ME > I have about three hundred of these so I'm really looking to make some trades here. There has to be something in my collection that you would like. Have a favorite animal? I even have some special edition ones like the millennium bear and Princess Di. They are in mint condition. Plus, they're really cute and would look great on a shelf in your living room or on your bed. These are rare collectibles, so while you may not think you have a need for them, they are really adding value to your home. Let me know what you think. Otherwise I can look around for some more stuff I have to trade.

PS - I will definitely take that blender.

SAM >

AGAIN, I DON'T REALLY NEED ANY BEANIE BABIES.

Happy to trade a blender but do you have anything else? Any furniture or art? I might also have a coffee maker in storage if you want to trade for it.

ME > Yes! I actually have a few little teddy-bear-sized benches and chairs I think I could part with. I used to pose some of my favorite beanies on them when I lived in my mom's house. I'll even throw in a beanie baby with each piece of furniture.

How does this trade sound to you:

1 Blender in exchange for 1 Blue chair + Ewey the Lamb (he fits perfectly in it)

1 Coffee maker in exchange for 1 Yellow mini wicker bench + Claude the Crab (he kind of takes up the whole bench)

Also have a number of clear display cases you can keep them in so they don't collect dust, if those interest you.

SAM > Ok, again, I don't want anything beanie baby related. Adult-sized furniture only.

If you don't want the blender or coffee maker just say so. I don't have time to negotiate in worthless stuffed animals.

ME > More like priceless stuffed animals, but I hear you loud and clear.

You mentioned you were looking for some art? I actually commissioned a few oil paintings a few years ago that are beautiful and one of a kind that I might be willing to trade. How new are these appliances, if you don't mind my asking?

SAM > They're probably 4 or 5 years old. What is the oil painting of?

ME > These are gorgeous oil paintings, let me tell you. One is a majestic underwater ocean scene of Coral. The other is a beautiful mountainous scene of Canyon. I am willing to barter both for those kitchen appliances. I was up until midnight last night looking up smoothie recipes.

SAM > Oh great they're of scenery? That would definitely be something I'd be interested in. Could you possibly send me a picture of them?

ME › Yes! I had them painted of two of my favorite beanies at the time, Coral the fish and Canyon the cougar. They are painted in beautiful nature settings and the artist even included their Ty beanie baby tags in their ears. Such detail, it's incredible. As much as I love these pieces, don't worry, I'm definitely willing to trade them for the two items we talked about. Question: does the coffee maker come with filters? If you could throw those in that would be great.

So how do you want to get these items to each other? I can have the art packed up tonight.

SAM › Wait, the paintings are OF beanie babies??? Are you serious??

I told you I didn't want them. I definitely don't want paintings of them.

DO YOU HAVE ANY ITEMS THAT DO NOT HAVE ANYTHING TO DO WITH BEANIE BABIES?

ME > They are set in nature, like I said when I originally described them, but I get it, you hate animals. I did a bit of digging and I found some other things I could trade you.

SAM > Of course I like animals - just real ones. Not beanie babies. What did you find?

ME > You drive a hard bargain but I really have my heart set on that blender.

I have a tabby cat named Sphinx that I would be willing to trade you in exchange for the two items we discussed. I think that's more than fair seeing as he is my pet. It was getting to be a little expensive having a pet in the city anyway and I trust you'll give him a good home since you claim to love real animals so much. I can send his litter box and scratching post as well since I will no longer be needing those. Since I'm throwing in all this extra stuff, is there a way you could sweeten the pot for me too? Do you have a microwave or toaster oven?

SAM > This is your actual live cat??? For a blender? Is this a beanie baby again?

ME > Ok, I'm a little confused here. Do you want a live animal or not? If it's a beanie baby you want, then please just tell me which one. There are several cats. There is Chip and Flip and Nip and Snip and Scat and Pounce and Prance and so on. Please be specific.

SAM > I don't want a live cat OR a beanie baby cat. I'm starting to think you don't have any items that I would want.

ME > All of that back and forth and now you want to call the entire thing off? Did you ever intend to trade me that blender at all or were you just wasting my time from the beginning? I could have stocked up my entire kitchen by now.

SAM > You have to be kidding me. I have actual items... you have beanie babies... and you are mad at me?

ME > I'm not mad. I'm disappointed.

SAM > I don't want your cat, I don't want your beanie babies, and I don't want your oil paintings.

ME > Ok does that mean you still may be interested in the clear display cases I mentioned earlier? They are not just for beanie babies, you can display anything you want in them... a signed baseball, some seashells, beanie babies... haha just kidding about the beanie babies.

SAM > No. Sorry I even responded to this ad. An unbelievable waste of time...

Looking for actor to play dead

I have a date this weekend and I'm looking for someone to come play dead in my apartment. All you should need is some makeup and a sheet to be a believable dead person. I'm not a necrophile or anything like that, so no reason to be freaked out. It's just a fantasy of mine to get sexy in the presence of a cadaver, so all you have to do is lie nearby to set the mood. It's roleplay really. If things go really well, there's a possibility you could be here kinda late. Just lie still until my date and I fall asleep—then you can collect your pay and let yourself out.

Salutations!

I'm a freelance actor with an interesting face and I've appeared in a variety of films, TV shows, commercials, webseries, and music videos. I've got lots of experience with comedic and dramatic improv, performance art, pranks, viral videos, etc. Perhaps I'd be a good fit for your unique project. Please find photos and resume attached.

ME ˃ That's great. Just a few questions. Have you ever played a corpse before? About how long would you say you could go without blinking? Would you mind timing yourself? We could probably go eyes shut if this ends up being an issue.

FRED > Thanks for reaching out! Funny you should ask—I've played a corpse several times, most notably as the "corpse of the week" on a CBS crime drama last season and in a Korean gangster film. I've attached photos of both "performances." I can go about 30 seconds without blinking, but depending on the lighting in the room, it might be best to keep my eyes shut.

ME > Nice, I love that show. Sometimes I watch those crime dramas to get myself hyped up for a date. Something about the stillness of the victims just puts me at ease.

Sorry but I have to ask, will you be able to stay in character during the aggressive love-making? Just want to make sure nothing breaks the mood.

FRED > Haha I can definitely stay in character, it would take an earthquake to move me.

ME >

THAT'S GOOD BECAUSE I'VE BEEN TOLD
I SOUND LIKE A WALRUS WHEN I'M
ABOUT TO CLIMAX. THAT'S AN EXACT
QUOTE FROM AN EX-LOVER.

We'll probably want you within about 6-10 ft of us so we can see you the whole time.

FRED > Haha gotcha! How long do you reckon that the lovemaking will go on? Of course I realize that may be hard to say in advance. :) And how much would the compensation be for the role? Thanks and cheers

ME > We'll probably have a few go arounds after dinner and drinks. Can't say for sure how long. We can discuss an hourly rate. Or if you'd prefer, I have a gift certificate to IHOP with $73 on it that you are more than welcome to. Who doesn't love pancakes, am I right?

FRED > I love pancakes but I love cash more ;) I could do $100/hr with a 2 hour minimum. Let me know your thoughts. Thanks and cheers

ME > Let's go with the pancakes for the first hour and 100/hr for the rest of the night.

FRED > I'd have to count on the $100/hr, any pancakes would be incidental and much appreciated. :)

ME > Fred, I'm gonna have to put my foot down here and ask that if I'm paying you $100 an hour that you keep your eyes open like a real dead person.

FRED > Haha fair enough! Of course I'll have to blink but I can make it quick and almost imperceptible. When are you trying to make this happen?

ME > I'm pretty nervous that the blinking might be too obvious and kill the mood. Can you use this week to practice not blinking? Here is a wiki-how I found that might help:

http://www.wikihow.com/Win-a-Staring-Contest

Hype man needed to boost my confidence before meetings

I've found recently that the more responsibility I'm handed at work, the more the pressure is slowly killing me from within. Last week I child-posed under my desk for an hour before bombing a presentation because I'm a juggernaut of insecurity and self doubt. I need a hype man to come give me the validation I need to succeed. "Hell yeah!"s and "That's right!"s. "You were born for this" is a good one. Don't be afraid to really get up in my face. Perhaps ask if various cities are in the house. I dunno. Put your own spin on it. Just get me amped up enough to go into my meeting and really kill it. No CV necessary, you just need to show me you can get me hyped.

I'll be your hypeman

ME > I have literal goosebumps. You sound like just the guy for this job. I've tried everything short of a hype man and I'm really hoping this works. Do you mind giving me a little taste of how you will pump me up?

KYLE > I'd hype you up by giving you a pep talk about how we are all mortal and YOLO is the way of life.

ME > Would you massage my shoulders while you tell me that as if I am about to go into the ring and fight?

KYLE > EXACTLY LIKE THAT! You got some high standards. I like it.

ME > Would you yell some stuff directly into my face to get me excited, like maybe something like...

YOU DA MAN! YOU DA BOSS! GO AND GET IT! YOU GOT THIS! GET IN THAT BOARDROOM AND KNOCK EM DEAD! YOU IN THE BUILDING!

YOU ON THE BLOCK! YOU OWN THE MOTHERF*CKIN BLOCK!!!!! ... I don't know maybe that's stupid.

KYLE > Absolutely.

NEW YORK IN DA HOUSE!!

WHAT ARE YOU WAITING FOR?! ITS YOUR TIME!

GO OUT THERE AND GET WHAT YOU WANT!

DON'T LET ANYTHING GET IN YOUR WAY!

YOU'RE A LEOPARD!

And many more...

ME > Ok that's more like it because for a little while there it felt like I was doing a lot of the leg work. I am very scared of leopards so please just keep that in mind when you're yelling the names of large cats at me. I have a huge meeting this Thursday afternoon. Would you please come to my office before to hype me up in person?

KYLE > Yes, I understand and will take in consideration your large cat phobia. You shouldn't be doing the leg work... Only leg work you need to worry about is ass kicking. I actually leave tomorrow for Florida.

ME > Of course you do. I am not meant for success. I might as well move to Africa and get eaten by a leopard.

THE NEXT DAY...

ME > Kyle, if you have not boarded your flight yet can you please send some motivation my way to get me pumped up. My boss would like to "have a word with me" this afternoon. I don't know what it's about, and I am under my desk crying.

Please get in-flight wi-fi if you can. Thank you.

KYLE > Oh man I just landed! How did it go?

ME > Horrrbylly. He told me I need to step up my performances or else. I'm at the bar..... why didn't you get the wifi??

ME > What song should I put on the jubekox

THE NEXT DAY...

ME > Kyle, send me your flight info, I want to get you onto a return flight that has wifi in case I need to get a hold of you.

KYLE > Hey man where are you?

ME > Calling off the search party man. Where have you been? I have a meeting in 30 min, could you swing by for a few???

KYLE > I'm in Orlando.

ME > Well, my meeting went horribly. You have not said a single motivational thing in days. What are we doing here Kyle? I'll be quivering under my desk if you're looking for me, which I doubt you will be, because you obviously don't care whether I keep my job or not.

ME > Seriously, Kyle?